George Henry Wakeling

King and Parliament

George Henry Wakeling

King and Parliament

ISBN/EAN: 9783337151669

Printed in Europe, USA, Canada, Australia, Japan

Cover: Foto ©ninafisch / pixelio.de

More available books at **www.hansebooks.com**

The Oxford Manuals of English History
Edited by C. W. C. OMAN, M.A., F.S.A.

KING AND PARLIAMENT

(A.D. 1603—1714)

BY

G. H. WAKELING, M.A.
FELLOW OF BRASENOSE COLLEGE, OXFORD

NEW YORK
CHARLES SCRIBNER'S SONS
1896

GENERAL PREFACE.

There are so many School Histories of England already in existence, that it may perhaps seem presumptuous on the part of the authors of this series to add six volumes more to the number. But they have their defence: the "Oxford Manuals of English History" are intended to serve a particular purpose. There are several good general histories already in use, and there are a considerable number of scattered 'epochs' or 'periods'. But there seems still to be room for a set of books which shall combine the virtues of both these classes. Schools often wish to take up only a certain portion of the history of England, and find one of the large general histories too bulky for their use. On the other hand, if they employ one of the isolated 'epochs' to which allusion has been made, they find in most cases that there is no succeeding work on the same scale and lines from which the scholar can continue his study and pass on to the next period, without a break in the continuity of his knowledge.

The object of the present series is to provide a set of historical manuals of a convenient size, and at a very moderate price. Each part is complete in itself, but as the volumes will be carefully fitted on to each other, so that the whole form together a single continuous history of England, it will be possible to use any two or more of them in successive terms or years at the option of the instructor. They are kept carefully to the same scale, and the editor has done his best to put before the various authors the necessity of a uniform method of treatment.

The volumes presuppose a desire in the scholar to know something of the social and constitutional history of England, as well as of those purely political events which were of old the sole staple of the average school history. The scale of the series does not permit the authors to enter into minute points of detail. There is no space in a volume of 130 pages for a discussion of the locality of Brunanburgh or of the authorship of *Junius*. But due allowance being made for historical perspective, it is hoped that every event or movement of real importance will meet the reader's eye.

All the volumes are written by resident members of the University of Oxford, actively engaged in teaching in the Final School of Modern History, and the authors trust that their experience in working together, and their knowledge of the methods of instruction in in it, may be made useful to a larger public by means of this series of manuals.

KING AND PARLIAMENT

(A.D. 1603—1714.)

CHAPTER I.

INTRODUCTION.

The Middle Ages had ended in England amid the storm and stress of the Wars of the Roses. Wearied out by thirty years of bloodshed on the battlefield and the scaffold, the English nation threw itself at the feet of Henry VII., and craved of him nought but "strong governance" and the end of anarchy. It was on these terms that he and his progeny ruled England. But the Tudors had a shrewd perception of the truth that Englishmen are more easily led than driven. They were tyrannical to many individuals who resisted their will in things secular or religious, but to the majority they represented that majesty and security which we now describe as the "State". For, while they maintained strict law and order in the land, as is the first duty of every government, they studiously avoided collisions with the prejudices and feelings of the nation. *The Tudor government.*

The result was that during the sixteenth century Englishmen developed a new spirit. It was not quite a spirit of liberty. We are accustomed nowadays to a freedom in our actions and opinions which was quite unknown then. If a man spoke or wrote or even thought differently from his fellows in Tudor times, he was suspected of disloyalty. There had been so much anarchy and division during the civil wars of the previous century, that an absence of disagreement was felt to be the all-important thing. *Led to a national spirit.*

The king and his government must be obeyed without

criticism. Religion was not, as now, a matter for each man to choose for himself without interference. The government could not afford to let men obey their own consciences. A Roman Catholic was an enemy of the nation, because he believed in the pope's authority rather than in the king's. A Puritan was suspected of disloyalty because he placed his own ideas before the law of the land. No one could be loyal both to pope and king: many had to choose between law and conscience. The slightest criticism of any matter in church or state was considered the forerunner of rebellion. If the Tudors gave England peace and order, they expected in return unquestioning obedience. The nation was to be one in thought and belief, for only so could it be one in action.

It was thus that Englishmen learnt to feel that they were one, and the sixteenth century gave us a national spirit. It was shown in many ways. Men like Raleigh felt sure that Nature intended Englishmen to fight Spaniards. Men like Richard Grenville expressed their joy that they "never turned their backs on Don or Devil yet". Shakspere transplanted into the tale of the Lancastrian reigns a fire and a patriotism which really belonged to his own day.

But the real source of this spirit was the change in religion. The Reformation had a profound effect upon England as a nation, and upon the separate individuals who composed it. It taught Englishmen to believe in their independence and freedom from the interference of the "Bishop of Rome". This was at the bottom of the great national feeling of which we have spoken. But men also learnt that since they are responsible to God for their own acts and words, they must learn to think for themselves. This was an entirely different feeling. It made each man believe in himself. It may be called the "personal" spirit. Now the Tudors wished to have the national spirit without this personal one. The first would help to secure reverence for their government, for men could see in the monarch the embodiment of that free orderly nation which was for

The double effect of the Reformation.

the future to depend upon itself. But the second was considered dangerous. It might lead men to question the sovereign's right to decide religion, as it had led them to question the pope's right.

Now this is exactly what happened. This personal spirit led men into a new religious belief. When in the latter half of the sixteenth century the Church of England, as established by law in Elizabeth's day, failed to satisfy some earnest thinkers, they adopted the extreme opinions of the continental Protestants. This new religious force was called in derision Puritanism. The men who held it wished to purify the church of all that reminded them of a hated Popish past—of bishops, of ceremonies and ritual, even of sacraments. Elizabeth, while relaxing wherever possible the bonds of discipline, yet refused to allow to individual consciences any departure from the church system she had established, either in the direction of Roman Catholicism or of the advanced Protestantism of the Continent. So the Puritans were punished for not conforming to the national church, no less than were the Roman Catholics. Some obeyed and accepted the Prayer-book and Episcopacy; others shook the dust of England from their feet and went abroad. Thus there were two new spirits or forces in the land which must some day become antagonistic to each other —the national and the personal spirit. The Tudor government had set itself to use the first and curb the second.

Puritanism.

At the beginning of the seventeenth century, therefore, England needed a great man, and there was a great work for him to do. When a nation becomes strong and united the time for absolute government is past. A monarch may act *for* a people when they are disunited, and discipline them when they quarrel, but he must act *with* them when they have learned the lesson of unity. They will then require some share in their own government, some right to advise or choose. They will refuse to be told what they are to do and believe, as if they were still unable to act and think for themselves. It is always a slow movement from the

Political danger of the time.

one form of government to the other, and at the crisis it needs a man who possesses the nation's confidence to lead it steadily along the path of toleration and self-government. Such a leader must believe in the nation no less than in himself.

The crisis had now arrived, and unfortunately for England the Stewart kings, who now sat upon the throne of the Tudors, were quite unfitted for the task. They believed in themselves and not in the nation. They thought they had a personal mission to govern, and consequently treated opposition and criticism as impudence or ignorance. No doubt they had a good deal of both to encounter; but the new rulers were unable to discern that, underneath the opposition and prejudices, there lay that spirit which has been the making of all great nations. James I. and Charles I. wished to work on Tudor principles, and failed to understand that they had to deal with a people which had already spent a sufficient number of years in the nursery. Nor were these kings prepared to work *with* the nation and take it as it was. They believed they possessed a "divine hereditary right", a right endorsed by their own wisdom and abilities, sanctioned by the personal power allowed to past kings, and upheld by their family tree. They did not comprehend that the sovereign power, which all efficient governments must possess, will only be respected by those who approve its work and can understand its methods. So they drew a line between themselves and the nation, and thus destroyed that mutual understanding which had supported the Tudor government. While the tyrant Henry VIII. had often taken his parliaments into his confidence, King James or King Charles were always careful to remind the Two Houses that they and their sovereign could never treat as equals. Thus the union of king and people which the Tudors had fostered the Stewarts neglected.

The Stewarts fail to meet it.

But the nation had learned the lesson and believed in it. When the good-natured laziness of James I. and the conceit of his son Charles allowed the national feeling to be wounded by arrogant Spanish ambassadors and subservient royal chaplains, resistance was aroused at once. In contemning the national spirit these kings aroused the personal one—the Puritan one. Roman Catholicism was still to most Englishmen the Evil One in disguise, and when the Stewarts refused to see it in that light, yet condescended to give no reasons for toleration, Puritan politicians were exasperated, while Puritan divines and pamphleteers wrote enthusiastic and wearisome tracts to prove that England was pledged to the continental form of Protestantism. High-Church clergymen were rewarded by royal favour for preaching and writing that the king was above the law, and could be neither criticised nor resisted. And the Puritans answered by combining their resistance to ecclesiastical "innovations" with a passionate claim for the supremacy of Parliament over the royal power. Thus the religious and the political opposition were merged in one. *[English Puritan spirit rises.]*

The struggle that ensued became a battle for "sovereignty", that is for the supreme and final power in the state. Both parties claimed divine sanction for their religious programme, and each wished the state to enforce it. The king and a majority of the churchmen combined to resist the claims of the Parliament and the Puritans. The Parliament and the Puritans combined to dispute the king's right to lay down the law in church and state. Thus the opposition, though it claimed to be national, was really inspired by that personal spirit which claimed the right to think for itself in matters political as well as in matters religious. Men began to teach that the real duty of a government was to get at the mind of the nation and carry out its will, rather than to dictate what was to be done and believed. *[Sovereignty at stake.]*

Now, the question of sovereignty was one on which it was useless to appeal to former practice; for there were enough precedents in church and state to justify both parties. Each accused the other of "innovation", or departure from custom, *[The respective arguments.]*

and each claimed the conservative position so dear to Englishmen. The king said that the claims of Parliament to a share in the sovereign power were unheard of, as indeed they were, if Tudor times were the test. Archbishop Laud thought the Puritan idea of a strict observance of the Sabbath was unheard of, which, until very recent years, it certainly was. On the other hand, Parliament considered that the king's claim to be above the law was unheard of, and on medieval precedents this too was true. The Puritans urged that the ceremonies they were told to observe were "innovations", and for many years this also was true.

The solution of the religious dispute was a gradual extension of freedom in thought and action, but for this neither party was as yet prepared. The solution of the political dispute was a gradual change of the form of government from one in which the king commanded and the nation chafed, into one in which the government was responsible to Parliament, while Parliament was responsible to the electors. The struggle wore on till it ended in war, which did not bring a settlement of the question. Not till the end of the century was toleration begun in practice, and the law finally placed above the king. But by the time of William III., the "Cabinet" responsible to Parliament, which carries on a national government in accordance with national wishes, was not far distant.

The real solution in the future.

When England had learnt that the majority of men in a civilized nation cannot be permanently excluded from a share in its government, the goal, to which the struggles of the seventeenth century had been pointed, was reached. It is our own fault to-day if we cannot trust each other in religious questions, and trust our elected government in national questions.

CHAPTER II.

THE REIGN OF JAMES I.: 1603-1625.

James Stewart, the successor of Elizabeth on the English throne, was the son of the famous Mary "Queen of Scots". He had been king in Scotland almost from his birth: on his accession to the crown of the triple kingdom, henceforth called Great Britain and Ireland, he was thirty-seven years old. His position in Scotland had been one of great difficulty, largely owing to the Presbyterian clergy, whose constant officious interference with him had grafted in his mind a firm belief in the merits of an Episcopal Church dependent upon the crown.

The new king.

James was acute in his own limited way, learned, and good-humoured; but his character was fatally marred by conceit, obstinacy, and indecision. His uncouth manners and ungainly person rendered absurd his claim to be considered a supernaturally-gifted king—the "British Solomon" as he loved to be called. An honest belief in his own abilities and good intentions is always a source of weakness to a man who has little power of work and less appreciation of difficulties. James was, and remained, without a policy, though a policy was imperatively necessary for one who had to deal with the two great questions which Elizabeth had left unsolved, the question of Sovereignty of the state, and the question of toleration in the Church.

The first ten years of this reign are marked by constant little failures which are hardly retrieved by the absence of any great mistakes. The king failed to keep in touch with his first Parliament, which lasted from 1604 to 1610, as completely as he showed himself unable to solve the increasing religious difficulties caused by the rise of the Puritans. In Ireland and Scotland attempts at a statesmanlike policy were thwarted by the royal obstinacy; but in foreign matters, where in after

Character of the first period.

days James was apt to flounder more than in domestic, he was kept from serious harm by the wisdom of his first minister, Robert Cecil, Earl of Salisbury.

The attitude of the Parliament toward the king was from the beginning ominous of troubles to come. The Commons stated in the "Form of Apology" (1604) that their privileges were their "right", not derived, as James thought, from the royal "grace". This strong language was occasioned by his attack upon the right of the Lower House to decide disputed elections. Nor did the leaders spare hints that the dangers of Elizabeth's reign had kept the Parliamentary demands more moderate than they were likely to be in future. The king merely replied that they should use their liberty with more modesty.

The feeling of Parliament.

The complete union of England with Scotland was one of James's dearest projects; but the English were jealous of Scots, and the matter was finally dropped because there was no agreement as to how it should be managed. Parliament wished to have a share in effecting it by legally naturalizing Scotchmen. This, the king thought, was accomplished by the mere fact of his accession. An appeal to the judges produced the decision that a child born in Scotland since 1603 was not an alien; and further than this the king, who had the best intentions in the matter, was unable to go.

The Scottish Union.

In religion, which was likely to prove the greatest *crux* of all, there were three parties: those orthodox Anglicans, who conformed to the Prayer-book and the Church system of Elizabeth; the obstinate few who remained true to Roman Catholicism; and the Puritans, who had been persecuted by Elizabeth, but hoped for better times under the new *régime*. The Roman Catholics were menaced by many laws passed in the late reign, which made the exercise of their religion high treason. They were also liable to fines for not attending their parish churches. The former are called the "Penal laws", the latter "Recusancy" fines. James did not share the bitter

The religious difficulty.

Policy to Roman Catholics.

feeling which had prompted these laws, and would fain have put an end to all religious quarrels. A noble aim; but not a practical one in an age when the Popes still looked upon England as probably reclaimable to the dominion of the Roman see. Parliament spoke the voice of the majority of Englishmen when it demanded the enforcement of these cruel laws. Their attitude was strengthened by the wild attempt of some fanatical Papists to sweep away king and Commons alike by the horrible "Gunpowder Treason". In 1605, these eager spirits—their chiefs were Catesby, Winter, Fawkes, and Digby—formed the "Gunpowder Plot". The Houses of Parliament were to be blown up during a sitting, at which the king and the Prince of Wales were to be present, by means of gunpowder placed in the cellars beneath. It was discovered through a letter in which one of the conspirators endeavoured to hint to his friend the danger of attending Parliament on November 5. After the execution of Guy Fawkes and others, persecution fell more stringently on the Catholics, for the nation suspected that they had all been implicated in the plot, and wished to exterminate the whole sect.

Meantime the Puritans were far from satisfied. In the Millenary Petition[1] presented to the king very shortly after his arrival in England (1603), they had asked for some alterations in the ceremonies to which all ministers had to conform. James arranged a conference between bishops and Puritan divines at Hampton Court. But there were great difficulties in the way of making the church wide enough to contain these men, who wished to modify the thirty-nine articles and to grant all presbyters a share in the Episcopal power. The high churchmen opposed all such changes. James himself had a wholesome dread of the introduction of the Scottish system. The only result of the conference was that some canons were drawn up in 1604, binding clergy and laity still more strictly to the Prayer-book.

The Puritans.

---

[1] So called because it was supposed to contain the signatures of 1000 ministers. As a matter of fact there were less than 800.

For the time the parliamentary protests against this attitude of church and crown were in vain. But when James showed a disposition to side strongly with church against state in matters of law, and proposed to settle the vexed question of the jurisdiction of church courts by hearing cases himself, he was led into a serious quarrel with Chief-justice Coke. The lawyer plainly told him that the royal power was official rather than personal, and that the Law was above it. Such a doctrine was anything but agreeable to one who held with "divine hereditary right".

Two theories of government.

Taxation was another point on which James was soon at issue with his subjects. The king's income was not sufficient for the needs of government as well as those of an extravagant court, whose officials made money at the nation's expense. Parliament was not liberal to a king with whom they so seldom agreed, and James, relying on precedents in the late reign, took upon himself to increase the import duties without consulting Parliament. Such "impositions" had been made illegal in Edward III.'s reign, but the judges decided in the case of Bate (1606) that the king could increase or vary such taxes by his prerogative or royal power alone. This was the first of a long series of cases during the century in which the king appealed to the Bench for a confirmation of his rights. James's first Parliament closed its seven years' duration with a quarrel over another financial difficulty. The "Great Contract" was a scheme by which the crown should renounce the antiquated feudal payments due from land in return for a fixed annual sum. This finally failed, for the Commons required, as a preliminary, satisfaction about "impositions" and church courts.

Parliament and taxation.

It was of little use for men like Bacon to hope that king and Parliament would work together for reform and progress. Each was in fact beginning to claim for itself a "discretionary power" to act somewhat beyond the existing law. The Tudor plan of doing what was necessary was losing credit in the face

No real hope of harmony.

of the further question of what was right; and it is certain that a man like James put a great strain on the idea that kings govern because they know best.

Meanwhile Ireland had its own set of difficulties and problems. The Irish rebellion of 1598 had been pitilessly crushed, and in 1604 Sir A. Chichester undertook the government of Ireland. There were two chief difficulties, land and religion. The native Irish looked on Protestantism as a foreign creed forced on them against their will. The Lord Deputy tried conciliatory measures, and hoped to educate the Irish in the change of faith. But the Irish Parliament of 1613 proved as intractable as the English, and James foolishly recalled Chichester, of whose moderate policy he had not approved. The agrarian difficulty, which Chichester had proposed to solve by abolishing the ancient Irish custom by which the whole tribe held the tribal lands in common tenure, and making the natives free tenants, led to a wholesale eviction of the latter and the colonization of Ulster by English and Scotch settlers. *[Chichester's rule in Ireland.]*

On the Continent the government had inherited from Elizabeth a policy of war with Spain, but as Spain was no longer dangerous James and Cecil wisely made peace (1604). There was, however, a feeling in England that something should be done for the Netherlands, that is, the countries we now call Belgium and Holland. The northern or Dutch provinces had recently thrown off the yoke of Spain, while the southern or Belgian had by cruel persecutions been kept back in their servitude. James was in fact induced in 1609 to guarantee, on behalf of the Northern provinces, a treaty by which they obtained a twelve years' truce from Philip III., but he refused to be dragged into a war against Spain in their interest. He also allied himself with Henry IV. of France, and with the Protestant princes in Germany, marrying his daughter Elizabeth to the Protestant Elector Frederick of the Palatinate. Such was the policy of Cecil, who died in 1612. With his death, following on that of Henry IV., and of James's *[Foreign politics. A Protestant policy.]*

hopeful son, Prince Henry, the chances of a successful foreign policy came to an end.

From 1612 to 1619 James fell from bad to worse. Finding that Parliament could not be moulded to his will, he came to rely on favourites who moulded him to theirs. He opened an intrigue with Spain, and became a tool in the hands of its quick-witted ambassador, Sarmiento, Count of Gondomar. He adopted Bacon's fatal theory-that-the judges should be "lions under the throne", *i.e.* the king's tools, and dismissed the Chief Justice, who objected to be made the exponent of this experiment in natural history. He trampled on the Scottish Church, quarrelled with the Dutch, and so lost touch with his people that when a national question arose in the last period of his reign he was unable to avoid disaster.

Second period of the reign.

A Scotchman named Robert Carr, upon whom James lavished titles and favours, was now his chief adviser. He had been made Viscount Rochester, and shortly became Earl of Somerset. The Spanish party at court, and the Spanish ambassador, Sarmiento, used this favourite to further their policy. The alliance with France had failed after the three deaths before mentioned, and the efforts of Spain were now directed to replace it by a closer friendship with the court of Madrid. The Spaniards had a delusion that Protestantism was merely an English fad, which might be removed with patience and care.

Carr and the Spanish party.

James's own idea was expressed in the words "*beati pacifici*". He loved to dream of himself as the peacemaking arbiter of a docile Europe. But he failed to see that Spain liked peace for other reasons; that she did not want England to help the Dutch, and was only trying to win toleration for the Catholics, fondly dreaming of the complete conversion of England to crown her castle in the air.

The king's aims.

The financial needs of the government caused a Parliament to be summoned in 1614. But the new assembly refused to supply the Royal needs unless it could obtain

THE FALL OF CHIEF-JUSTICE COKE. 13

some satisfaction about "impositions", which had been largely increased since the case of Bate.[1] The Spanish party suggested that a marriage of Prince Charles, now heir to the English throne, with the wealthy Infanta Maria, daughter of Philip III., would settle James's debts; and the king, relying on the kindly feelings of the Spanish ambassador, dissolved Parliament after two months. Digby, afterwards Earl of Bristol, was intrusted with negotiations of a vague character for the Spanish match. He was able and honest,—too honest to be on a level with the Spanish diplomatists.

The "Addled Parliament".

The obstinacy and consequent dissolution of Parliament soon caused another return to arbitrary taxation by royal mandate. This took the form of a "Benevolence" or free gift, but the gift was in truth so little free that a man named Oliver St. John was prosecuted in the Star Chamber for refusing to contribute. This court, the king's favourite engine, was extremely powerful, because exempt from the ordinary rules of judicial procedure. It had been very effectual in suppressing disorder in Tudor times, and was now composed of the members of the Privy Council, who were thus able to punish those who resisted the royal authority. It was practically the ministry sitting as unfettered judge of its own acts. It was not long before the crown gained a further ally in a subservient Bench. Chief-justice Coke had an exaggerated opinion of the importance of the lawyers, but his belief in the law was a useful weapon against a king who claimed to be irresponsible. He disagreed with Bacon's idea, and considered that the judges should be arbiters in the state, a view which would only suit James so long as they arbitrated in his favour. When, therefore, Coke asserted his duty as a judge to act, not on the king's orders, but as the law dictated, he was dismissed (1616). Bacon became Chancellor soon after this, and the Stewarts had little further trouble from independent judges.

Law and Prerogative.

The Dutch were driving James further in the direction

[1] See page 10.

of a Spanish alliance by disputing the English monopoly of whale-fishing, and excluding them from trade with the Spice Islands in the East Indies. But the arrogance of Somerset was unbearable, and his anti-Spanish opponents were already undermining his monopoly of the king's favour, by teaching a handsome, clever youth named Villiers to attract the king's notice. At this moment the Spanish conditions of marriage were announced, and as they included a suspension of the Penal laws and a Catholic education for the future heir to the throne, the hopes of the opposite party revived. Their triumph appeared even more sure after a scandalous lawsuit, in which Somerset and his wife were pronounced guilty of poisoning a courtier named Overbury, who had known some damaging facts about the divorce of Lady Somerset from her first husband. James, however, was not easily diverted from his hankering after Spain. He feared the nation's feeling might develop into a war-cry, and apparently thought he could allay their prejudices by selling their laws and opinions. The enemies of Spain had now found a ready weapon in the old Elizabethan sea-captain, Sir Walter Raleigh. He had been in prison for twelve years for supposed complicity in a plot against the king. But he was still eager to sail to the Orinoco and discover a mine of gold of which he had heard in former voyages. James allowed him to go, though the Spaniards cried out against the scheme as an infringement of the unlimited rights which they claimed in the West Indies. Raleigh, though warned not to trespass on these rights, started with no intention of keeping so impossible a promise. After an unsuccessful voyage, in which his men fought with Spanish settlers and burnt St. Thomé, he returned to find the king pledged to hand him over to Spain. The disgrace was avoided, but Raleigh was sacrificed to Spanish hatred, and executed in 1618 on the old charge of treason, which had kept him so many years in the Tower.

The new favourite, George Villiers, had now become the king's trusted adviser as Duke of Buckingham, but did not at once throw in his lot with the Spanish party. This, and the fact that the Infanta and her dowry could not be obtained without complete toleration of the Roman Catholics, caused a suspension of the marriage scheme. But the king, though he ceased for the time to bargain for the sale of the conscience of England, showed but scant respect for that of Scotland. He called an Assembly at Perth (1618), which was forced to adopt Five Articles, prescribing rites and ceremonies to which the Scottish clergy and people strongly objected. It is to be noticed, however, that James never went so far as his less prudent son, and made no attempt to enforce uniformity of worship in his two kingdoms.

Meanwhile the European horizon grew dark with the great shadow of the Thirty Years' War. This struggle began in Bohemia in the year 1618, and aroused the national feeling in a way that made it more than ever necessary that there should be a leader with clear aims and the confidence of his people. But the last period of the reign, from 1618 to 1625, presents a pitiable spectacle. A helpless king, drifting aimlessly amid a sea of conflicting interests, without a policy which he dared to explain to the nation, was content to seek for guidance from the bitterest enemy of the nation —Spain. *Third period of the reign.*

The struggles which had begun during the last century between Protestants and Catholics in Germany had been compromised but not settled. There were German princes pledged to each side, and each prince claimed to regulate the religion of his subjects. But latitude and longitude cannot really determine opinion, and if they could, it would be hard to settle what was to be done, when a ruler held sway over many lands of varying opinion. This was the difficulty which had now occurred. The Emperor Matthias, when dealing with his Bohemian subjects, was obliged to allow both religions. The claims of Protestants to build churches on Catholic church-lands led to the destruction of one of their places of worship, and the Protestants at once rebelled. The rest *The Thirty Years' War.*

of Germany was composed of states interested in one side or the other; but before much could happen the Em-
The Bohemian Election. 1619. peror died, and the Bohemians took the opportunity of refusing to accept his successor, the bigoted Ferdinand II. In August, 1619, they elected James's son-in-law, Frederick of the Palatinate, as their king. James believed in his family far more than in his country, and was anxious to prevent the loss of his son-in-law's domain on the Rhine, which would probably follow should Ferdinand be successful in Bohemia. But he believed even more in himself, and so he began to study the question of Bohemian rights while the time for action slipped away.

James had two choices. He might meditate or he might fight. For the latter alternative he had a thorough dis-
Mediation or War? like, and he was certainly wise in not wishing to embroil England in continental quarrels for the sake of a man like Frederick. This prince was proud and incapable, and went to Prague only to see his cause overthrown by the Imperial forces in Oct., 1620. But if James would mediate he had a fair chance. Spain, though connected by her Royal family and religion with the Emperor Ferdinand, was not at all eager to fight for the Catholic cause; as she was shortly expecting a renewal of her war with the Dutch. The Protestant princes were not anxious to see their religion trampled on, and the Palatinate transferred from Frederick to the Duke of Bavaria, which was the Emperor's intention. France, too, was bound to be jealous of Austro-Spanish success. Thus there was an opportunity both to defend the Palatinate in force, and to mediate in the matter of Bohemia.

While James was studying the question the Palatinate was seized. Thus the clever Gondomar had gained his
Parliament or Spain? 1621. object. James had relied on the high opinion he always held of Spanish kindness, and Buckingham had at last thrown in his lot with Spain. When the affairs of the nation had got quite beyond their control the Stewarts generally summoned a Parliament, and in 1621 James pursued this course. Here was a good

opportunity to put himself at the head of his people. He spoke of money which he needed to enable him to mediate "sword in hand", but, as he did not explain his intentions further, no money was voted. The truth was, he had no plans to explain. Parliament attacked the trade monopolies, which were sold to courtiers, demanded the execution of the Penal laws on the Papists, and begged the king to fight Spain and marry his son to a Protestant. While the Commons were showing the intensity of their feeling by cruelly punishing a Roman Catholic named Floyd for expressing pleasure at the defeat of Frederick, James and Buckingham were hoping to get back the Palatinate by the old delusion of the Spanish marriage. The king first promised Gondomar not to allow Parliament to offend the religious feeling of Spain, and then promised the Houses not to conclude any treaties which would be disadvantageous to the religion of England! When the Commons refused to leave the matter to the care of the king and the Spanish ambassador, they were told not to meddle with "mysteries of state". This, with a further declaration that their power to discuss national interests was derived from the royal grace, caused them to protest that their liberties were their birthright. The protest was torn from the journals by the angry monarch's own hand, and the third Parliament of King James was dissolved.

Meanwhile the war in Germany went on. The Protestant cause was in the hands of a reckless soldier of fortune named Mansfield, who was alienating friends by plundering and slaying the peasants of the Rhine districts. The Protestant Union gave up the struggle, and the saving of the Elector's cause was rendered hopeless when Heidelberg, his capital, fell in September, 1622. The "intervention" of Spain, on which James had relied, was as far off as ever; and the Spaniards, having now secured their object, were inclined to finish the negotiations by pleading the impossibility of obtaining the Pope's assent to the marriage.

Failure in the Palatinate.

At home James was without a single wise counsellor.

Digby was in Spain trying to construct a policy out of Spanish politeness and his master's fears. Bacon, the Lord Chancellor, had fallen a victim to his own carelessness in accepting presents which can only have been meant as bribes, and was in disgrace. Buckingham and the Prince, over whose weak character the quick and reckless favourite had complete influence, now determined to go to Spain and arrange the marriage themselves. James was induced to assent to this absurd scheme; but his council preferred to send an ultimatum to Spain asking whether Philip would fight the emperor to force the restitution of the Palatinate. This brought a deceptive reply, but it showed the Spaniards that their game was nearly played out.

A new project.

The situation when the travellers reached Madrid was remarkable. The king, Philip IV., and his ministers, as well as the Infanta herself, were all in reality averse to the match. James never meant to promise the repeal of the Penal laws, and the Spaniards never meant to take less. Charles imagined that he was in love as soon as he saw the Princess, while Buckingham offended all the Spaniards he could offend in the short time given him. The Pope refused to be made the cause of a rupture of which the Spaniards meant him to bear the blame, and Philip IV. found it impossible to propose any terms which Charles was not foolish enough to accept. Even after bargaining to obtain a repeal of the Penal laws in three years, the Prince still failed to carry off the prize, and left Madrid in a fit of ill-temper.

The visit to Madrid. 1623.

When he was home again his pride outweighed his affections, and he called for vengeance on the Spaniards. He was still pledged to the marriage, but it was now England's turn to raise the terms, and Philip was asked to arm against his family and his religion to secure a restitution of the Palatinate. The dilemma was in fact so hopeless that another Parliament was summoned for February, 1624. Buckingham and Charles were able to pose as national heroes, who had burst the chains riveted by Spain to fetter English freedom.

Parliament of 1624.

The treaties were dissolved and money voted. But the chance of acting with Parliament speedily vanished.

Buckingham now became anxious for an alliance with France, the old foe of Spain, and wished to secure the hand of a French princess for Charles. Parliament was more than ever determined to keep to the Penal laws, and in foreign affairs to renew the work of Elizabeth and smite Spain by sea and land. The King of England was thinking only of the Palatinate, and was as willing to rely on French charity as on Spanish, but hated all idea of a religious war. The French were delighted to see Spain injured, but cared nothing for the Palatinate, since they were only bent on recovering the Valtelline, the Alpine valley by which the Spaniards had an access to Germany from the Mediterranean. Nor was France sufficiently in need of the English alliance to waive her claim for toleration of Roman Catholics in England. *A hopeless confusion of politics.*

The result of this confusion was soon apparent. James, having given a clear promise to Parliament not to repeal the Penal laws, thought that he could still write a secret "engagement" with France, by which the Roman Catholics were promised toleration. The marauder Mansfeld was hired to lead English troops to recover the Palatinate, but when they crossed the sea they were left to die in hundreds of cold and hunger on the Dutch frontiers. The marriage treaty with France, however, was duly signed, and the French king was promised assistance against his rebellious Protestant subjects. While Buckingham, who still retained the unmerited confidence of the nation (won on his return from Spain), was thus unwittingly concocting a series of national disgraces, the king died on March 27th, 1625. He was only in his sixtieth year, but his unhealthy habits and hard drinking had made him old and decrepit long before his time. *Result of the confusion.*

CHAPTER III.

THE REIGN OF CHARLES I. TO THE MEETING OF THE LONG PARLIAMENT: 1625–1640.

From the accession of the second Stewart king in 1625 until the meeting in 1640 of the Parliament which was to arm half England against him, there are three well-marked periods. Till 1629 there is a constant struggle with three successive Parliaments which refused to finance the kaleidoscopic foreign policy of the king and Buckingham. From 1629 to 1637 the rule of the king was absolute. He summoned no parliament, he taxed as he pleased, he legislated by proclamation, he bent the judges to his will, and gave Archbishop Laud *carte-blanche* to mould the church to the extreme High-Church and anti-Puritan model; while Strafford in Ireland reproduced on a smaller scale the same tyrannical form of government. The nation seemed quiet, and all fear of resistance to the Stewart methods appeared to be at an end, when Scotland rose in rebellion in defence of its religion. The three years' struggle that ensued completed the period. In 1640 there was no hope for Charles but in an English Parliament, and on Nov. 3 the long struggle began for the sovereignty of England.

<small>Three divisions of this period.</small>

The new king was married to Henrietta Maria, sister of Louis XIII. of France, in June, 1625, but her influence was at first slight compared to that of Buckingham. Charles was a prince of a quiet and sober disposition: he possessed all the private virtues, and was an enlightened friend of art and letters, but he had learnt only too well his father's doctrine of the infallibility of kings, and he was so obstinate and so convinced of his own good intentions that he scarcely understood the necessity of saying exactly what he meant and meaning exactly what he said. His word could never be depended upon. He was easily led

<small>Charles and his councillors.</small>

into a sudden action, and easily "amazed" when he was committed to it. Thus his policy at home and abroad was marked by impulse rather than by thoughtfulness. He disliked intolerance, but used it when it suited any policy which he had in hand. Indeed he seems to have thought that even deception was a fair weapon to gain ends which he believed to be just. Yet he was a loving husband and father, a hard-working man of business, and a fairly staunch supporter of his friends. His greatest fault as a king lay in the fact that he did not in the least understand men. He considered that all those who disagreed with him must be wicked rather than mistaken, and must be forced to see things in the right light. The same fatal flaw was in his friend and adviser, William Laud, whom he made Archbishop of Canterbury in 1633.

Sir Thomas Wentworth, afterwards Earl of Strafford, who, after a brief resistance to the court in Parliament, joined the king's party because he found himself out of his element among Puritan members, was a third believer in the necessity of carrying through the opinions he held, no matter what resistance was offered, a method which he called the policy of "Thorough". These were the three men who were soon to exasperate England, and bring Scotland and Ireland to open rebellion, not because they wished to harm any one, but because they did not know how to lead men who refused to be driven.

Before his first Parliament met, Charles and his favourite were resolved to fight Spain. But Louis of France was quite unwilling to give any active help, and England, besides engaging in the new Spanish war, was also pledged to assist the Dutch, pay large sums to Mansfield, and subsidize the Danish king, who was now posing as the champion of Protestantism in Germany. The first Parliament showed its distrust of the king, to none of whose confidences it was admitted, by refusing to vote a tax on imports and exports, known as "tunnage and poundage", which had for centuries been granted to kings on their accession as a matter of course.

Parliament of 1625.

Their Puritan sentiments were also outraged by the encouragement of those clergy who openly taught the king's superiority to law, and maintained extreme high-church doctrines. In the end the leaders began to single out Buckingham as the chief cause of troubles. This was an attempt to make a royal minister responsible to Parliament, and though there were many precedents for it, yet it was so opposed to Tudor practice and Stewart theory that Charles dissolved Parliament in the same year. At once the favourite and his master resolved to show their ability by an attack on Spain. They sent out an expedition, which sailed into Cadiz harbour in October, 1625, but it turned out a complete and disgraceful failure.

A second Parliament found this expedition an additional grievance. Sir John Eliot, Vice-admiral of Devon, led the attack, and the favourite was impeached. This, again, was more than Charles would permit, and the Houses were dissolved after demanding the dismissal of Buckingham as an enemy of church and state.

Parliament of 1626.

The French alliance was becoming too great a strain on Charles's temper. He was vexed that the ships which he lent to his ally were used against the rebellious French Protestants at La Rochelle, though it was for this very end that Louis XIII. had borrowed them. He was annoyed by the claims of his wife to regulate her household, and he dismissed her French attendants. He was of course quite unable to fulfil his promises to tolerate Roman Catholics, and in 1627 a war with France was the natural result. Buckingham started to attack the island of Rhé, from which Rochelle was menaced.

War with France. 1627.

The expedition, however, proved an even more dismal failure than that of Cadiz, and Parliament met in 1628 to present an ever-increasing list of grievances. These now take clear shape. The exaction of forced loans and benevolences, the imprisonment of men by the Royal power alone, the billeting of recruits in private houses, and the use of martial law, were de-

Parliament of 1628.

clared to be against the rights of Englishmen; and Charles, after some attempts at resistance, was compelled to agree to this "Petition of Right".

But it was not only in political matters that Parliament was determined to make a stand. They complained bitterly of the "Arminians".[1] This was a name given to Laud and his high-church friends, who were carrying the king with them in their resistance to Puritanism. They refused to acquiesce in the extreme forms of Protestantism which had been for a long time in force on the Continent, and to which the Puritans wished to bind the English church. This development of Protestantism was called Calvinism, from the French reformer Calvin, who had led the movement in the sixteenth century, and whose teaching had been largely accepted in Switzerland and other places. One of his chief tenets was "Predestination". He taught that God had once for all chosen His elect by His mere will and pleasure, and to the number of those there could be no additions. This was felt by many to be opposed to the idea of a merciful God who called upon men to repent and accept salvation. English churchmen resisted this Calvinism, and maintained that the teaching and ceremonies of the English church were to be looked for in her history, and that she could repudiate the errors of Rome without needing the hard teaching of the extreme Reformers. But the fact that the Churchmen firmly believed that the Commons were only resisting the king for their private ends, and were encouraged by Royal favour to say as much, complicated the religious difficulty by making it political.

The "Arminian" grievance.

In the summer of the year 1628 Buckingham was assassinated at Portsmouth while preparing an expedition to relieve the Huguenots in Rochelle. An officer named Felton, who grew angry at not getting promotion, brooded over his wrongs, and began to attribute them to the man who was spoken

Charles against Parliament.

[1] So called from Arminius, a Dutchman, who led the opposition to Calvinism in Holland.

of in Parliament as the enemy of his country. He was at last driven by such thoughts to the terrible crime of murdering the hated duke by stabbing him. The king was thus left to conduct his own government. The way seemed open for a better understanding. Much might have been done now, for the Houses would have welcomed any attempt to work with them. Pym, the future parliamentary leader, and Eliot, the future martyr to liberty, were alike anxious to see king and Parliament in harmony. Not a word had been said against Charles personally. Even a Puritan writer, who did not scruple to describe the bishops as "knobs and wens and bunchy popish flesh", had a kind word for the "good, harmless king".

But Charles was dogmatically sure of his path, and insisted on his right to levy tunnage and poundage without *Religious and financial grievances.* grant, holding that it was not included in his renunciation of "gifts, loans, taxes, or benevolences" in the Petition of Right. The leaders of the House encouraged merchants to refuse payment. They were also thoroughly alarmed at "innovations" in religion, and determined to put their case before the country. Three resolutions were passed, declaring those who introduced religious innovations, paid tunnage and poundage, or exacted it, to be enemies of the country. The Speaker, who wished to abscond, was meanwhile held in the chair by excited Puritan members, and the doors locked to prevent the dissolution which they knew to be imminent, and which followed as a matter of course.

The king now determined to rule without Parliament, and for eleven years he managed to get along somehow *Absolute rule. 1629.* without one. Eliot and others were imprisoned for their recent action in the House, and the judges were induced to refuse them liberty unless they acknowledged their fault and promised amendment. This was refused by some, and Eliot died in prison three years later.

Peace had of course to be made with France and

Spain (1630), and though Charles had a fine opportunity for recovering the Palatinate he was obliged to refuse it. Gustavus Adolphus, King of Sweden, the greatest warrior of the age, carried all before him in Germany; but the English king had no power to back him, and the Protestant champion fell on the field of Lützen in 1632. Yet, Charles was not inclined to abandon his sister's cause. In 1633 he returned to his father's futile hope, and actually allied with Spain against the Dutch in order to get Spanish help in the matter of the Palatinate. He required a fleet, and revived an old custom by which maritime counties were obliged to supply ships and money in time of danger. As he dared not announce his Spanish intrigue, even to his council, he issued his first writ of Ship-money in 1634 on the plea that channel pirates must be put down. The fleet sailed about the channel but accomplished nothing, and as France and Holland now combined against Spain there was small hope of her intervention to secure Charles's family interests in the Palatinate. *[side note: Foreign policy and Ship-money.]*

In 1633 two events of profound import occurred. Wentworth was made Lord Deputy of Ireland, and Laud succeeded Abbott as Archbishop of Canterbury. For seven years Ireland was ruled by a fearless and strong hand. Wentworth knew that it required both. "Where I found a church, a crown, and a people spoiled, I could not imagine to redeem them with gracious smiles and gentle looks. It would cost warmer water than so." This was his own account of his prospects, and he certainly followed it out. In a few years he modelled and disciplined a standing army, cleared the coasts of pirates, introduced some manufactures, started the growing of flax, and reformed the church system. But he forgot to be careful about the means he used. In order to get land for colonists he violated some concessions known as the "Graces", which had secured the native lords against such possible confiscations. He brushed aside legal and constitutional rules as easily as he crossed the ideas and customs which *[side note: Wentworth and Laud.]*

centuries of use had endeared to the people. His objects were noble, his achievements were great, but his lasting success was *nil*. He won no hearts.

What Wentworth sought in Ireland Laud sought in England—unity by means of enforced uniformity. For both the lever was the Royal power. For both the watchword was "thorough". Laud used the Star Chamber and High Commission Court to force Englishmen into a groove. He spared neither rank nor creed. He wished to punish the immorality of the rich, the nonconformity of the Puritan, and the recusancy of the Roman Catholic. The object, unity, was as noble as Strafford's, but the methods were as fatal to real success. Laud wished to see the Church one in the "Beauty of Holiness"; one in belief, one in ceremonial, one in resistance to Romanism. {.margin: The Laudian system.}

This was impossible. There were good and holy men who were unable to agree with him, and there were also those whose scurrilous language and irreverent ways were a legacy from the fierce struggles of the early days of the Reformation. Some of these ardent Puritans, disappointed at the failure of the Millenary Petition and Hampton Court Conference, had already left their country to seek a new home where they could worship without interference. These "Pilgrim Fathers" sailed in the *Mayflower* (1620) to the shores of North America. Here they formed a colony, soon to become the great state of New England. Among those who remained at home, there was a feeling that the outward forms, to which the Archbishop exacted conformity, were really a pathway to Rome. Thus men refused to bow at the Sacred Name, to kneel at Holy Communion, to use the Communion Table anywhere but in the centre of the church. Though we can now acquit Laud of any desire or intention of being untrue to the national church, there were not wanting signs which led honest men to think otherwise. A papal messenger was long at the court on friendly terms with king and ministers. Roman Catholic converts were sure of the {.margin: Twofold resistance.}

queen's protection, and the chapels of her majesty and the foreign ambassadors were neutral ground. If this was only tolerant we must not forget that it was also illegal, and to the majority of Englishmen incomprehensible, except on the basis of a deeply-laid scheme to restore the church to the Pope. Men were imprisoned, whipped, pilloried, and mutilated for libels on the bishops. Of these victims the best known is Prynne, who had already been punished by the Star Chamber for a book condemning stage-plays, which was thought to contain some aspersions on the theatre-loving queen. In 1636 he was a second time pilloried, and the remains of his ears shorn off.

The national feeling was shown by the open sympathy which such men received. But there was no sign of a cessation of the system. In 1635 Ship-money was demanded in a second writ which extended the tax to inland counties and towns. *Sovereignty of king or of nation?* The king consulted the judges and published their answer, which declared that he could legally order such payment, and "was the sole judge of the danger" which justified such unusual demands. But it was clear there was no immediate danger. The nation required a defensive system for which Parliament might easily have been summoned. To pretend that a discretionary power, which is necessary in an emergency, had become part of the ordinary law of the land, was to raise the question whether Parliament was more than a name in England. The freedom of the nation was at stake.

In 1636 a third Ship-money writ followed, and a gentleman of Buckinghamshire, named John Hampden, whose contribution was assessed at twenty shillings, determined to refuse payment and have the matter tried in a law-court. *Would England submit?* His counsel took their stand on ancient laws, concluding with an appeal to the Petition of Right, and urged that no man was bound to pay taxes except when granted by Parliament. The judges, however, adopted the theory that the king had a right to command, since he was the soul of the body politic, and by a narrow majority gave judgment for the crown. Ship-money was not the only means taken by Charles to fill his coffers and avoid a Parliament. Ancient forest rights were revived, and men were fined for infringing them; compulsory knighthood, a relic of the feudal age, was revived, and fines demanded for exemption; monopolies were granted to companies, since a law of 1624 forbade them to individuals; and the customs were collected and increased, though, as we have seen, they had never been granted to Charles by Parliament. Yet, the king seemed secure in his course. There were no newspapers, railways, or meetings to make the national disgust articulate. Nothing but a Parliament could focus the religious and constitutional opposition to the system of "thorough", and since the king was determined to avoid all foreign complications there seemed no prospect of such an assembly being summoned.

The blow which shattered this system came from Scotland. James had irritated the Presbyterians by his bishops and ceremonies, but Charles did worse. He visited Scotland in 1633 and gave the bishops a footing they had never had before. They were promoted to political office, and the chief power in the Scottish Parliament. This sent even the nobles, although they feared and disliked the democratic Presbyterian clergy, into the arms of the kirk. But worse was yet to come. Laud and his master were determined to unite England with Scotland in religion as a step towards complete political union. To this end canons, which enforced a new Prayer-book and a ceremonial foreign to the Scottish Church, were prepared in 1636. Charles had already been warned not to "import a servitude on this church not practised before", but he knew not the meaning of a nation's feelings. When in 1637 the new service book appeared it was described as the "Mass in English", and a riot occurred in July when it was introduced at St. Giles's in Edinburgh.

The Scots' resistance.

Charles had at last roused a resistance which was national. The Scots nobles, clergy, and people, with

very few exceptions, refused to admit that their religion could be touched except by national assent. And they did not need to wait for a Parliament to express their meaning, for the very nature of Presbyterian organization was political. *Covenant and Assembly. 1638.*
Each parish had its "kirk-session", whose representatives sat in the Provincial Synod; while the whole church met in a National Assembly, where laymen and clergymen attended on behalf of every congregation. A church so organized could not be tampered with. Petitions poured in from the parishes, commissioners were elected to meet in Edinburgh, and in 1638 a *National Covenant* was ready for signature. It pledged the Scots to resist all popery and innovations, and was signed by high and low. An assembly met at Glasgow which scouted the king's attempts to check its action, and swept away at one blow Episcopacy and Perth Articles.

Charles, having no standing army, was not ready with the weapons of force: he began to temporize. His offers to modify the position he had taken up were refused; the Scots, now fully roused, would be content with nothing less than an acknowledgment of their absolute freedom in religious matters. *What would Charles do?* The difficulty before the king was great. He had no army, no money, and no friends. The English feeling during the three years of struggle was largely in favour of the Scots. Laud was mobbed in London, and a daring hand placarded the Royal Palace "to let". The Scots knew how to avail themselves of this, and more than once appealed to the English nation. There were two plans before the king. Wentworth wrote advising a delay of hostilities, fortifying of the border, blockading of Scottish ports, to "keep the blue bonnet to his peck of oatmeal", and careful training of a force for action in the coming year. But this could only be done if money were forthcoming, and there was little hope of that. The king determined on war. The Scots were ready. They had collected a large force at Dunse, on the border, under a veteran soldier, Alexander Leslie, and their historian Baillie describes them as constantly preaching, praying, and drilling. Puritanism had become the church militant. What had the English king with which to meet this enthusiasm?

Pacification of Berwick and the "Short" Parliament. He rode to York and on to Berwick, but the forces which had been got together were both badly disciplined and half-hearted, in marked contrast to the rebels a few miles off. In June, 1639, a verbal treaty was made at Berwick, in which no real settlement was made, and a General Assembly and a Parliament promised to the Scots. When these met in August they demanded the abolition of Episcopacy and a veto on the king's appointment of commanders in the Royal castles. Charles, failing to see that he was expected to play the part of a conquered enemy, at once accepted Wentworth's proposal to rely on his English Parliament. After eleven years' silence the representatives of England met again in the Short Parliament, April 13, 1640. They sat for three weeks. Pym stated the feeling of the nation when he claimed for Parliament that position as "the soul of the body politic" which Charles had so long claimed for himself. The grievances of eleven years were put forward and discussed. The king attempted to rouse enthusiasm against the Scots by exhibiting a letter addressed "Au roi", which the latter had, perhaps, intended to send to the King of France. But this seemed a trifle compared to the three writs of Ship-money. Parliament was clearly not to be moved to abandon its claims. Nor would it give the government a penny to fight with, and the inevitable dissolution followed on May 5, 1640.

Strafford's programme. This time Wentworth, now Earl of Strafford, wished for no delay. He gave his advice at a meeting of the Privy Council, in which he urged the king's right to go on with the war, "loose and absolved from all rules of government". "You have an army in Ireland," he is reported to have added, "which you may employ here to reduce this kingdom." Though this speech was to cost him his life, which was even now in danger from a terrible disease, its import was greater for his country than for himself. Once before Strafford had urged the

A SCOTTISH VICTORY.

king to govern England as he had himself been ruling Ireland, and the conviction that Charles meant to do so was to grow until it severed the nation into two hostile camps.

On August 20, 1640, Charles left London, and the Scots, who were again ready to fight for religious independence, crossed the border on the same day. This time there was no hesitation: they forced a passage of the Tyne at Newburn on the 28th, and occupied the Northern counties, the Royal army gradually falling back before them. *Second Bishop's war and Treaty of Ripon.* The king, being without money or means of obtaining a reliable force, summoned a Great Council at York, which could only suggest a Parliament and a fresh negotiation with the rebel Scots. At Ripon the king agreed to pay the latter £850 a day while they remained in England, which they meant to do until they obtained a peace and religious settlement after their own wishes. Thereon commissioners were appointed and the negotiations were to be re-opened in London.

Strafford's advice had not been followed. All classes of Englishmen, from the peers at York to the 'prentices in London, were at last fully roused. While the former urged the necessity of reliance on Parliament, the latter tore down the posters which proclaimed the Scots as rebels. *The king's lesson.* It would have been well if the king had now been convinced that no reliance on a man, or a theory, or a party can enable government to conquer a national spirit which it will not lead. But this was a lesson Charles never learnt, though his failure has taught it to succeeding ages.

CHAPTER IV.

FROM THE MEETING OF THE LONG PARLIAMENT TO THE COMMENCEMENT OF THE CIVIL WAR: NOV. 3, 1640—AUG. 22, 1642.

When the Long Parliament met on Nov. 3, 1640, there was among its members no clear plan of action, and certainly no idea of rebellion. There was an almost universal feeling in favour of a thorough reform, not of the constitution, but of that which contemporaries call the "state of the kingdom". But it was to be done *with* the king and not despite him. King and people, it was said, needed each other, and "reciprocation is the strongest union". The interest of the first period is to watch the collapse of this noble ideal as soon as it became evident that the two conditions, trust and mutual understanding, were wanting.

Reform with the king.

The first object was to vindicate law and restore the rights of Parliament. "We are assembled to do God's business and the king's," said a foremost speaker: this meant doing away with Strafford's influence and Laud's power. Accordingly they were both impeached, together with others who were responsible for arbitrary acts. This challenge to the power above the law was marked by the release of Prynne and others imprisoned by the Star Chamber and High Commission Court. The "Triennial Act", providing that a Parliament should meet even without a Royal summons, after three years had elapsed since it last sat, was then passed.

Early measures of Reform.

The trial of Strafford was delayed till March, 1641. He was accused of an intention to upset the rule of law and replace it by arbitrary government. Besides many acts and sayings, in Ireland and in his Northern Presidency, alleged against him to prove this, there was his speech in the Privy Council, in which he was accused of telling the king to govern as he

Trial of Strafford.

thought best, there being an army in Ireland which could be used against "this kingdom". Now, "this kingdom" might mean Scotland, which was then in rebellion; but it might also mean England, and the Commons felt sure it did. It was difficult to prove that the acts of which he was accused were treasonable, for they were not in any way directed against the king; and the law knew nothing of any other treason. The expression of an opinion might, as Strafford urged, make a heretic but not a traitor; and the two witnesses required by law to depose their knowledge to treasonable acts were not forthcoming, unless, indeed, a surreptitious copy made by the younger Vane of the notes taken by his father, a member of the Privy Council at the fatal sitting, could be reckoned a sufficient second witness. The Commons began to fear that the Lords would not condemn Strafford, and therefore substituted a Bill of Attainder.[1] This only required a majority of opinion that Strafford was a traitor, and thus shifted the question from a legal to a political one. The Commons held a noble theory of treason: "Treason which is against the kingdom is more against the king than that which is against his person": but this was not law. Some of them claimed to be above the law in such a crisis. They were beginning to learn that the theory of Divine right was double-edged, and might be claimed by parliaments no less than by kings. The bill was passed, and the Lords were induced to accept it by various rumours (not without foundation) that the king's party was tampering with the army in the north. Charles signed it—it was the meanest moment in his life—and gave away the life of his faithful servant, though he had pledged his word to Strafford for his safety: but Charles was influenced by mobs without and by casuistry within. The former threatened the lives of those he held dearest, while the latter taught him to regard his duty as a king as unconnected with his promise as a man. Strafford died

---

[1] An impeachment is a trial before the Lords, in which the accused has his chance of defending himself: an attainder is a mere declaratory bill stating that the accused has committed treason and shall be punished for it.

on Tower Hill, May 12, 1641. At the same time a bill was passed that this Parliament should not be dissolved without its own consent. This exceptional guarantee for its political stability was necessary if Parliament was to regain its position after eleven years of non-existence. The ground for a reformed system of law and government was further cleared by the abolition of the Star Chamber, the High Commission Court, and other extra-legal courts in Wales and the North. The most sacred principle of the old constitution was vindicated by the reversal of the Hampden judgment on ship-money, and by a clear surrender of the royal claim to take customs without Parliamentary consent.

Charles now appeared to have given in, and the reform seemed complete. But at this moment he announced his intention of going to Scotland, which might mean further intrigues with the army. Pym and the leaders saw this would not add to the harmony upon which the new state of things depended, and cleverly united the Lords and Commons, who had shown signs of disagreement, by the production of a document called the "Ten Propositions". These asked the king to disband the Irish and English armies, to delay his journey, and to put his affairs in the hands of those whom Parliament could trust. For the moment, however, little notice was taken of this motion, and when Charles departed for Scotland in August, 1641, a suspicious but still united Parliament was left behind him.

The king will not act with Parliament. June, 1641.

Suspicion was to increase, unity to diminish. So far the Parliament had been completely successful both in clearing the ground of the instruments of arbitrary government and in consolidating their own position: law had been restored, and the legislature vindicated. But the supreme object, reform *with* the king, had failed: he was not in touch with the Parliamentary leaders, and it was clear that they must base their further progress on support outside their walls.

The beginning of disunion and revolution.

For this the ground was already prepared, but it involved the danger of a split among themselves. To understand this we must go back and trace the gradual formation in Parliament of a church party prepared to resist the Puritan extremes which Pym allowed to his followers. This is of vast importance, for, though there was now no court party to be reckoned with, any violent action inspired by Puritanism would rouse a church party which would sooner trust the king than allow the church to be pulled down. *Disunion.* Early in the session there had been an animated debate on a petition to abolish Episcopacy, some wishing to consider it, others, while willing to modify the power of the bishops, being averse to any idea of abolishing the office. A "Root and Branch" party, pledged to destroy Episcopacy, was thus face to face with men like Hyde and Culpeper, who were opposed to such extremes quite as much as to arbitrary government. The Commons had issued a commission to deface and demolish crucifixes and images, while the House of Lords had appointed a committee to discuss ecclesiastical innovations with a bishop in the chair. The Scots commissioners in London were working against Episcopacy, and there was a strong and growing feeling that Scots had no right to meddle. The London citizens might present petitions against Episcopacy "in their best apparel", but many felt, and one member said, that "a parity in the Church" must lead to a "parity in the Commonwealth". It was thus clear that if Pym and his party put the church question in the front rank the unanimity against the king would be at an end. They did so, nevertheless.

There was therefore a considerable reaction in favour of Charles at the end of 1641; he had given way to all demands, he had surrendered his old advisers, he had gone to Scotland with no bad effect on the English army; the bishops were not without their supporters; the Scots were not everywhere popular, and there was a feeling that the "lads at Newcastle" had been the mainstay of the rapid Parliamentary success since October, 1640. *Charles gains by this disunion.*

The Commons precipitated a split on religion by an

ordinance (Sep. 1641) against the Laudian ceremonies, and the Sunday sports. The Lords replied by ordering the services to be conducted in accordance with the law of the land. This gave Charles a chance, and he seized it. He took up this attitude of obedience to law and announced that he would maintain the Church as in Elizabeth's day.

Further religious division.

But Charles never knew how to play his own game even when he had winning cards. An event in Scotland increased the suspicions of Parliament. The "Incident", as it was called, arose from a quarrel among the Scottish nobles. Montrose was opposed to the democratic form of government for which Covenanters under Argyle were striving. Hamilton was intimate with Argyle, and Montrose offered to prove him a traitor; a plot was formed by certain other nobles to arrest and carry off Hamilton and Argyle, and it was rumoured that Charles was concerned in it. This was not at all likely, but his motives in going to Scotland were suspicious, and it was believed in England that some such attempts were contemplated against English leaders. Parliament voted for itself a guard to be placed round the Houses, though members who were estranged from the majority on church matters ridiculed this alarm. It was clear that the split in Parliament was complete, and that Charles would have a party to depend upon and a cause to maintain.

Suspicions increasing. Oct. 1641.

The Irish rebellion, which broke out in 1641, attended with horrid massacres of Protestants, brought matters to a head. It was at once said that Charles and the queen were concerned in this rising of Roman Catholics against Protestants. There was immediate need of action to suppress it. Parliament had been taking upon itself to issue ordinances without Royal sanction during Charles's absence, and now sent to Scotland to tell the king that, unless ministers approved by Parliament were appointed, they would be compelled to take measures for the safety of the kingdom without him. This was a revolutionary challenge. Distrust had culmi-

An ultimatum to the king.

nated in an ultimatum. What would be the attitude of the non-Puritan party? This was soon to be tested. The situation was clear. The Parliamentary leaders, unable to act with the king in a reformed government, had given him the choice of acting with them or being neglected.

Such a situation was at once seized by Pym in the "Grand Remonstrance"; this re-stated all past grievances from the accession of Charles, and concluded with a fresh demand for ministers whom "Parliament may have cause to confide in". It was a bold appeal to the nation against the king. The Remonstrance was carried by the narrow majority of 11, and the split in the Long Parliament was complete.

The Grand Remonstrance. Nov. 22, 1641.

Charles had now returned from Scotland, where he had recklessly yielded to demands without obtaining a party on his side. Once in London he set to work to court popularity, made a foolish speech at the Guildhall, referring to his favour with all but the lower classes, and withdrew the guards of the House of Commons. In his answer to the Remonstrance he took his stand on the strict letter of the law; he would support government in church and state as it was established. This gave no security for that Parliamentary control over the king's ministers upon which Pym and his followers were set. How far suspicion carried the constitutional leaders may be seen from the fact that their next step was a bill to transfer to the Houses a share in the control of the Militia—the only armed force known to the ancient law. Charles did his best to justify these suspicions by appointing a notorious bravo called Lunsford to the most important military post in England, the command of the Tower; yet, a moment after, he cancelled the appointment in deference to the outcry it caused. The bishops, who had been mobbed on their way to the House, protested against the legality of all that took place in their absence, and Charles approved their action. There was a motion in the Lords that Parliament was not free, and there was a fear that the king would repudiate his past concessions and punish the Parliamentary leaders.

Charles's action increases distrust.

Finally Charles made the blunder of impeaching five members of the Commons and one peer "for endeavouring to subvert the fundamental laws of the realm, to deprive the king of his power, and to alienate the affections of the people from him". It was quite illegal to do this, as the king cannot impeach. But Charles went further. When the impeachment failed he made the irreparable mistake of going himself to the House with an armed retinue and trying to seize the persons of the "five members", Pym, Hampden, Holles, Hazelrigg, and Strode. Warned in time, they had left the House, and Charles had to retire amid cries of "privilege". The king had put himself hopelessly in the wrong.

The Militia question now became a real one. Parliament was disinclined to admit any power in the king to call out the local forces of the country, and demanded that all fortresses and the militia should be confided to men whom it could trust. This Charles would not grant, and an ordinance for the disposal of the militia was drawn up by Parliament. Men were named in each county to train and order the force. This was finally agreed to by both Houses, and the king had already decided to retire from London. It was evident that both sides were now preparing for war. The Parliament had the courage of its convictions, and as Charles would not act with the leaders, they took measures for the defence of the kingdom. Hull was ordered to be guarded, the port of Portsmouth was closed, the Tower was besieged, and the magazines all over the country were secured.

Preparing for war. 1642.

The question now was whether any one would fight for a king who had proved the suspicions entertained of him to be well grounded. Appeal was made to the nation by both parties during the early months of 1642 in a series of vigorous manifestos.

Appeals to the nation.

Charles took his stand on his legal power as king. He would not be "swaggered into any more concessions". He would maintain the church intact, though he signed a Bill for removing Bishops from

The king's attitude.

the House of Lords. But there was also the Divine right of himself and his family; he would not give up "the power he was born unto", nor prejudice the inheritance of his successors. This was a strong position. It attracted all those who feared democratic government, who loved the church, or who believed it a sin to rebel against the will and person of the king.

If Charles solved the problem of sovereignty by an appeal to his pedigree it was impossible for the Parliamentary leaders, now that they had gone so far, to stop. Their own solution, to which they had been gradually led, was a startling challenge to the king's. They claimed to be the interpreters of the national will, to which the king's will must finally bend. He was an officer, not a despot. The kingdom was not his property, but only the sphere of his trusteeship. "The judgment of Parliament," they declared, "is the king's judgment, though the king in his person be neither present nor assenting thereunto." *Parliamentary casus belli.*

There remained no solution but war, which began with a series of races for the possession of the local magazines of arms, that of Hull for instance. Hull was, moreover, a strong post, in a loyal district within easy reach of Scotland. Charles, on demanding admission, was met by the answer that Hull could only be opened to those who possessed the king's orders "signified" by Parliament. Here was the new theory put into practice. Parliament issued the Militia ordinance, and began assembling trained-bands in London. The paper war, to which reference has been made, came to a head on June 2, 1642, when the "Nineteen Propositions" were presented to the king at York. They placed him in the position of a figure-head to the constitution, and were by his friends called "Articles of Deposition". Charles replied by issuing "commissions of array", and began to assemble troops. The Earl of Essex, a taciturn soldier, with a stern sense of duty, some experience, and not a spark of genius, was made general of the Parliamentary forces. True to their conception of sovereignty, *Taking measures for war.*

the leaders raised soldiers who were "to live and die with the Earl of Essex for the defence of his majesty and Parliament". The king's standard was hoisted at Nottingham on the 22d of August, 1642.

The cause of the Civil War has been much in dispute. Was it a religious or a political struggle? The answer is *Religion or Politics?* clearly that it was both. The gradual sundering of king and Parliament as the various questions arose has been shown. The question of government was insoluble, because every moment the breach between the two theories of the constitution grew wider. There was no compromise possible. But the nation might have found a better way had there been no religious severance. Puritanism and its organization had been used as an engine to coerce the king, and thus his party was made possible. "Let religion be our *primum quærite*," said a speaker in November, 1640. The question of government and sovereignty had, however, been the real one, and religion had served to accentuate differences which might otherwise have been almost unnoticed. His majesty's will as expressed by Parliament was in conflict with his majesty's will as expressed by himself, and this difference was rightly placed in the forefront of the Parliamentary programme. The question of religion was to regain its importance, and provide the enthusiasm with which Cromwell and Fairfax would beat the king when their less zealous friends, the mere political reformers, had grown tired of fighting for a cause which they did not understand.

CHAPTER V.

THE CIVIL WAR TO THE KING'S DEATH, 1642–1649.

When war was thus declared neither party had a powerful army, a definite plan of action, or a sure *Division of England.* hold on any large tract of the country. But, roughly speaking, it may be said that the North and West

TAKING SIDES. 41

favoured the king, while the East and South, immeasurably the richer half of England, adhered to Parliament. Yet there were local struggles in which divisions appeared inside these limits; and along the border-line between East and West, in Yorkshire, Staffordshire, Leicestershire, Warwickshire, Berkshire, and Hampshire, there was plentiful division.

The king could reckon on the strong loyalty which was still felt for his person and for the cause of the church among large numbers of the nobility, gentry, and peasantry. Parliament was sure of a few similar adherents, and of the whole of the middle classes in the districts which held to them. But there was this important difference. The Royal cause centred round a person, the Parliamentary cause round a principle little understood and vaguely enunciated. Further, in the Parliamentary cause there was this difficulty—what was the real aim of the war? Was Charles to be beaten in the field and forced to terms, or pursued and punished? This is what made the rebel position so awkward. There was no clear understanding of the object of the war. The vow "to live and die in defence of king and Parliament" did not sound a very thrilling cry when those who uttered it were fighting with one but against the other. The king, on the other hand, had a clear end to pursue, the conquest and subjection of Parliament, for which was needed only a victorious march to London. *Prospects of the combatants.*

Thus the struggle was sure to develop in one direction. The king must attack, and the rebels must defend, the line which divided their respective strongholds. Every accession of territory for the king would be therefore a step nearer his end, but for Parliament attention must be concentrated on defence. Even if they beat him Charles was still king, and no one knew on what terms Parliament would lay down their arms. This course of action, defence by Parliament and attack by Charles, was made even more necessary by the fact that the former had no reliable permanent force. Too many of the Parliament's adherents were willing to fight a *Nature of the struggle.*

campaign with the clear object of barring the king's progress to London, or relieving a besieged garrison; but they were sure to flag when the effort was over. "The Londoners, as is their miskent custom, after a piece of service, get them home," says the Scots commissioner.

Meanwhile the war had definitely commenced, with some advantage to the Parliamentarians. Goring, who **Early fighting in 1642.** held Portsmouth for the king, surrendered it early in September, and thus put an end for the present to any hope of a strong southern position for the Royalists. The Marquis of Hertford had been placed by Charles in command of his forces in the South-west, but was stoutly resisted. He succeeded in getting possession of Shepton-Mallet, but was besieged on taking post at Sherborne, and failed to make any stand in these parts. He went, therefore, into Wales, sending his lieutenant, Sir Ralph Hopton, to Cornwall.

The central struggle of the year was between the king and the main Parliamentary army under Essex. The latter **Edgehill. Oct. 23, 1642.** assembled at Northampton and pressed on towards Nottingham, where Charles had but a small force. The king determined to march westward and recruit his ranks among his adherents in Wales. On his way from Shrewsbury to Chester he gained large reinforcements. Essex followed and occupied Worcester, though Prince Rupert, the king's nephew, a dashing, reckless cavalry officer, won a skirmish at Powick Bridge, in an endeavour to save it. Having at last gathered a host of some strength, Charles started for London on October 12. Essex followed and came up with him on the slopes of Edgehill, not far from Banbury. The Royal forces had to leave a strong position on Edgehill to make the attack. Rupert at once charged, drove the enemy's cavalry before him, and pursued them for five miles, leaving the king to fight with infantry only. These were practically without leadership, for the king possessed courage without military skill. The Puritan foot-soldiers in Essex's army behaved splendidly, and their conduct was matched by that of the king's "Red Regiment". Sir Edmund Verney died with the

THREE ROYALIST CENTRES. 43

Royal Standard in his hands, and the Earl of Lindsey, the king's general-in-chief, was taken prisoner, mortally wounded. When evening came the Royalist position was still maintained, though Rupert returned to the field to find that his reckless pursuit had turned a victory into a drawn battle.

Charles had so far the best of the encounter that he was able to go on to Oxford after taking Banbury. There had been some conflict in Oxford, where the loyalty of the University was not shared by the townsmen; but now it was to become the king's chief stronghold and head-quarters during the rest of the war. The way to London was open, and the advance began in November. The citizens expected an attack. When Rupert had sacked Brentford, the whole militia of London marched out to Turnham Green to oppose the Royal army. Charles, not inclined to risk a battle with 25,000 citizens fighting to save their hearths and homes, retired to Reading, and finally to Oxford, thus throwing away his hopes of success. *The march to London.*

There were now three chief gatherings of Royalist forces, the king's head-quarters at Oxford, Hopton's small force in Cornwall, and the Northern Royalists under Newcastle, fighting for supremacy in Yorkshire. These three centres must be separately watched during the next campaigns. *Royalist successes till August, 1643.*

In the centre there were many small encounters, chiefly owing to the endeavours of the rebel commanders to stop communication between various Royal forces. Essex took Reading, and established himself on the east side of Oxford, where he was attacked by Rupert and his cavalry. The engagement at Chalgrove Field (June, 1643) is chiefly noteworthy owing to the death of Hampden, the hero of the old dispute about the Ship-money, who was mortally wounded during the skirmish. The Queen landed on the Yorkshire coast with arms and money from Holland, and the Royalist successes in the Midlands, where they took Tamworth, Lichfield, and many other towns, enabled her to get in safety from York to Oxford. *In the Midlands.*

In the North Newcastle had some difficulty in holding his own against Lord Fairfax and his son Thomas, York-
Newcastle in the North. shire magnates who were vigorous for Parliament. He penetrated as far as Pontefract after beating Lord Fairfax at Tadcaster. As Newark was held for the king it would have been easy for him now to join Charles, but he preferred to turn his attention to the reduction of the West Riding. His advance was checked by the younger Fairfax, who recovered a part of the county for Parliament. This was, however, retrieved by a victory over the two Fairfaxes at Adwalton Moor (June 30, 1643), which once more turned the tide in the North. Hull alone held out for Parliament. To utilize this success by an attack on the enemy's forces in the Eastern counties was Newcastle's next project. This, however, was not well carried out, and the Eastern Roundheads, under Colonel Oliver Cromwell, who now first appears on the scene, were able to beat the Royalists at Gainsborough. Cromwell came of an old Huntingdonshire family, and had been in Parliament as early as 1628. He was already giving proofs of those qualities which were to raise him to the foremost place in England. While others hesitated Cromwell always acted, and knew how to adapt means to ends. While so many in Parliament and in the field were far from sure as to their aims and methods, this man of clear views and quick action was a power indeed. To common sense and tact he added all that was most vigorous in Puritanism, a firm belief in Divine guidance, and a keen sense that a great cause was intrusted to him and his "lovely company", as he called his grim Puritan troopers.

Meanwhile, in the West of England, the king's troops had won a series of brilliant victories. Hopton, assisted
Hopton in the West. by the local gentry, among whom the Grenvilles were conspicuous, made himself master of Cornwall. He won a clear victory at Bradock Down in January, and was then confronted by Lord Stamford, who came from Wales to aid the Western Roundheads. The departure of Stamford to the West had set Hertford

free to join Charles at Oxford with his Welsh recruits, and when he had taken Cirencester, all the Severn Valley, except Gloucester, was in Royalist hands. Sir William Waller was now sent as Parliamentary general to the West, and by his "nimble marches" secured Bristol, Monmouth, and Chepstow, and surprised Hereford. Meanwhile, Charles was writing to Hopton in Cornwall, bidding him push on to Oxford. Hopton had again beaten Stamford at Stratton and "taken in" most of Devonshire. This had to be stopped, and Waller came from Wales for the purpose. It was no light task, for there were already Royalist troops at Salisbury ready to join Hopton: their junction was effected at Chard, and in two combined attacks on Waller at Lansdown and Roundway Down they were completely successful. The result of these successes was the surrender of Bristol, then, and for long after, the second city in the kingdom.

Thus in these six months of 1643 there had been an almost uninterrupted series of Royalist victories. With Newcastle supreme in Yorkshire and Hopton in the West Charles had no force to fear. This was the moment for striking a final blow on his enemies by concentrating all his forces on London. But it was impossible. Hopton and Newcastle reported that their troops "utterly refused" to leave their homes exposed to attacks from rebel garrisons. Charles himself had a "miserable army" for such an attempt, and the chance was abandoned when it was decided to attempt the siege of Gloucester instead of taking advantage of the dissensions in London. *The crisis. August, 1643.*

There had indeed been during this period a growing desire for peace. The extreme Puritan party had no part in it, but the Lords and the City of London, together with several counties, were anxious to send terms to the king. The Commons had *Treaty of Oxford. Feb. 1643.* to assent, and proposals hardly less stringent than the Nineteen Propositions were sent to Oxford in February, 1643. Charles sent counter proposals, demanding restoration of ships, forts, and revenue, protection for the

Prayer-book, and a disclaimer of the right to tax and imprison. There was no hope of agreement, though the fruitless negotiations dragged on for months.

The determination of the king to besiege Gloucester called forth an enthusiasm on the part of his enemies to relieve it. Essex's resolute eight days' march with 8000 Londoners through a hostile country was one of the boldest strokes of the whole war. *First Battle of Newbury. Sep. 20, 1643.* On his approach Charles abandoned the siege, intending to cut off the enemy's return to London. After an unsuccessful attempt to outmanœuvre Essex the Royalist force followed him in the direction of Newbury. The Parliamentarians had taken the Kennet-valley road to London, and to occupy Newbury was the only chance of barring their passage. Essex and his men fought their way on from field to field only to find the open country stoutly held. Two regiments of London trained-bands resisted the shock of Rupert's cavalry and behaved "to wonder". The Royalists lost some of their noblest. Lord Falkland, sickened by the sights and sounds of civil war, courted and found death. A whole day's fighting left the Royal position still unforced; but during the night the king, being short of ammunition, abandoned his posts, and Essex reached Reading in safety. The year's fighting was brought to a close by the successes of Hopton, who led his Western army as far as Arundel, Winchester having been already surprised, and Dartmouth surrendered to Rupert's brother Maurice. In the eastern counties Lord Manchester had been placed in command by the Parliament, and his second in command, Cromwell, had grasped the truth, that enthusiasm, equal to that of the Cavalier gentlemen, could only be secured by enrolling Puritans who would fight with "a spirit". His new levies soon proved their worth by defeating the Royalist cavalry at Winceby. [October, 1643.]

With the commencement of 1644 two important changes must be noticed. The Scots had been induced to send a force into England on the Parliamentary side, and Charles had made a treaty with the Irish *Allies on both sides.*

leaders, by which he had already obtained an increased force and hoped for more. The "Solemn League and Covenant" entered into by the Scots and the Parliament in September, 1643, was, from the Scottish point of view, an alliance for the establishment of Presbyterianism in England, but the English looked little further than the assistance they were likely to afford in the war. The Irish "Cessation", September, 1643, was a twelve months' truce with the Catholics in Ireland, which would enable Charles to bring over his *English* troops, the wrecks of Strafford's old army, and use them against Parliament.

The "Solemn League and Covenant" was Pym's last triumph. His death in December, 1643, removed the great leader who had kept a majority together during the critical days of religious difference in the Long Parliament, and who, though no theologian, had placed the Puritan programme in the van of the Parliamentary position. He believed in Puritanism as a national force. Death of Pym.

But the Westminster Assembly, where a settlement of religion was now being debated, was beginning to show a line of division between Presbyterians and Independents, which was, later on, to wreck the cause of Puritanism in England. Difficulties were occurring too in the Royalist camp. There were quarrels among the commanders, many of whom, like Prince Rupert and his brother Maurice, objected to civilian influence exercised by such men as Hyde and Culpeper. Charles had gathered a counter parliament at Oxford— his "mongrel Parliament", as he called it—which also caused trouble, as his conduct in Irish affairs was not popular among the English gentry. But it gave the king's cause a great show of legality, as it included more than half the House of Lords, and a third of the Commons. Division in both camps.

Similar contentions were arising in the eastern counties and among the Parliamentary commanders. Essex and Waller were jealous of each other, and Cromwell was anxious to bring forward in the army the Independent Puritan elements which he had seen to be of such

BALANCED SUCCESS. 49

splendid fighting quality. Thus, with Irish intrigues, military dissensions, and religious bitterness, the intervention of the Scots, who were anxious to convert England to the opinions they held on Presbyterianism, only threw one more question on the table—the "divine right" of presbyters and elders to rule church and control state.

Early in 1644 Hopton's successes received a rude check by his defeat at Cheriton, in Hampshire. Newark was also in danger, and there were indications that Newcastle would be hemmed in by the Scots from the North and by Cromwell from the East. The loss of the North would be a crushing blow to Charles, who was unable to concentrate his forces to relieve Newcastle, as he was now met by a combination of Essex and Waller. They approached Oxford at the end of May. Rupert was sent with the best of the king's troops to relieve York, into which Newcastle had retired, and Charles remained in the Midlands with the rest of his host to deal with his two foes.

Dangers in the North and centre. 1644.

Fortunately for the Royal cause Essex and Waller elected to act separately, and the former went south to relieve the few seaports which held out in Devon and Dorset from local assailants. Charles had now to fight Waller, and succeeded in checking him at the engagement of Cropredy Bridge. Waller's troops were clamouring to get home, and thus Charles had no difficulty in marching after Essex, who actually retired into Cornwall in the end of July, and allowed himself to be hemmed in by the king. His army surrendered at Lostwithiel, but he himself escaped by sea to Plymouth. [September, 1644.]

Royalist success in the West.

Meanwhile, this success of the king in the West was more than balanced by the entire loss of the North. Here the Scots had joined the Fairfaxes and the troops of the Eastern Association under Manchester and Cromwell, for the siege of York. Rupert had carried all before him till he outmanœuvred the Parliamentary generals and reached York. Joining Newcastle's forces he advanced close to the enemy on the

Loss of the North.

slopes of Marston Moor on the evening of July 2. The rebel forces at once attacked. Cromwell's cuirassiers and Leslie's dragoons broke up Rupert's cavalry, though Goring routed Fairfax on the other wing, and the Scots in the centre were terribly pressed. But Cromwell defeated Goring as he returned from the pursuit, and Leslie succoured his countrymen in the centre. Finally the Royalist infantry fell back, and a complete victory for the rebels dealt a final blow to the king's hopes in the North. But in this perplexing war local struggles were raging everywhere.

There was no unanimity even in Scotland. The Marquis of Montrose, who was opposed to the idea of a Presbyterian democracy, placed his hopes in Charles; and with the astounding belief that Presbyterianism on an aristocratic basis could be achieved for England and Scotland by helping the Royalist cause, he now raised a Highland force and prepared to strike a blow for the king. He won some wonderful victories, beginning with Tippermuir in September, 1644, and by the middle of 1645 his successes seemed as if they might have a serious effect on the ultimate event of the war. *Montrose in Scotland.*

After the great victory of Marston Moor there is no doubt that vigorous action on the part of Parliament might have gone far to stop hostilities and bring the king to terms. Charles had to get back from the West, and if the rebel forces could have concentrated rapidly enough, it would have been possible to bar his passage to Oxford and pen him in the western peninsula. The army of Essex was dissolved, but Waller was sent to hold Charles in check, and Manchester was ordered to go to the "West" to support him. Manchester, who is described as a "sweet, meek man" by the Scotchman Baillie, had no taste for crushing the king in person; while Cromwell, his lieutenant, the "darling of the Sectaries", felt that this was precisely what was wanted. His troopers, who fined each other for swearing, and sang their psalms before throwing themselves on the Royalist cavalry, would have followed him *The Parliament's chance.*

against any foe, spiritual or political. The result was, that, in spite of the necessity, and the eagerness of some, Manchester asked for a definition of the word "West", and delayed to co-operate with Waller. This was fatal. Charles, having given his foes time by waiting for levies, arrived near Newbury on October 22, 1644. Waller had fallen back and been tardily joined by Manchester and Cromwell. The Parliamentary cause was not advanced by the action of the "Committee of Both Kingdoms", a body in whose hands military matters had been placed since the arrival of the Scots in England. They gave orders from London, and instead of placing one man in command and giving him a general's freedom of action, they had on this occasion appointed a council of war to manage the campaign. The result was shown in the battle that ensued at Newbury.

The Royal forces were strongly posted, and it was decided to attack them in the rear by a flank movement. *The chance is lost. Oct. 27, 1644.* To make success certain the main body was to divert attention by attacking the Royal position in front. A party under Cromwell and others successfully stormed the rear of the king's position at Speen. But Manchester hesitated to make the attack in front, and when he finally did so, late in the day, he was repulsed. Darkness put an end to the struggle, and Charles's forces got safely away towards Oxford. The prey had escaped.

Both sides had now lost a great opportunity, and both had learnt the lesson. Organized forces and determined *The lessons of failure.* leaders must be obtained for Parliament if they were to beat the king. The Royal forces must leave Oxford to itself, and crush their foes in detail, as they could not yet get to London.

Meanwhile, the Parliament had begun to organize the "New Model Army", a permanent Puritan force, which was ready early in 1645. The "Self-denying Ordinance" excluded all members of Lords and Commons from command, and left military power in the hands of a proved soldier, the younger Fairfax.

Hand in hand with this reform came the execution of Archbishop Laud (June 10, 1645), and the further severance of Presbyterians from Independents. The latter wished for toleration and state supremacy over the church, the former for the systematic enforcement of Presbyterian methods and no state interference. The Independents believed in themselves, while the Presbyterians believed in a system of church government. There was a weighty third party, at whose head was the great lawyer Selden, which dissented from the extreme views of both Independents and Presbyterians, and meant to uphold state control over both. Yet the growth of the Independent party was on the whole steady. The Scots were keenly averse to this new form of Puritanism, and began to hope for something from Charles; hence the fruitless negotiations which took place at Uxbridge in January, 1645. The Independents smiled and went on with the New Model. *Religious divisions.*

In the spring of 1645 Rupert went to Wales to recruit, and hoped to be joined by Charles. The two would attack the Scots, who had been obliged to send large forces to the North, where Montrose was wasting Argyleshire. Cromwell, with a handful of cavalry, made a dashing raid round Oxford, and carried off the horses, without which no guns could leave the Royal head-quarters. By this time the New Model was ready, and though Rupert had joined the king, Fairfax was ordered to relieve Taunton. This was a mistake, for it left Charles free to fight the Scots. While he was endeavouring to find them, Fairfax, abandoning the relief of Taunton, came back to besiege Oxford. If the place had been stronger the king might have beaten the Scots and joined Montrose, who was carrying all before him. But Charles, after sacking Leicester (May 31), feared to go too far from his southern stronghold, and Fairfax was therefore able to bring him to battle. Charles was at Daventry, and the Royalists neither knew nor cared anything about the New Model army. The despised Parliamentary forces surprised the king near *The king's plan.* *Naseby. June 14, 1645.*

the village of Naseby on June 14. Again Rupert dashed off the field after making a brilliant charge. Cromwell and his troopers were thus enabled to turn the scale in favour of the Parliamentary infantry, and the king's army was completely beaten and its infantry cut to pieces.

Charles's cause was now almost hopeless. Enthusiasm and organization were on the side of his enemies. Their quarrels were laid aside, and the real victory rested with the Independents. The Royal intrigues with the Irish and with foreign powers had been discovered by the capture of the king's cabinet at Naseby, and proofs of his machinations were on view in London to convince doubters. His commanders were quarrelling, or, like Goring, drinking away his cause in the West.

Failure of the Royal cause.

The real weakness of the king's position was that he was safe nowhere. His foes now realized that he must be closely followed and prevented from raising another army. He was in Wales in July, but the Scots were making it untenable, and the king's hope was in a junction with his western forces. In the West, however, the New Model, after its victory in the Midlands, was engaged in a brilliant campaign which made Parliament masters of the Devonian peninsula. After Fairfax's victories at Langport and Bridgewater in July the only ray of hope was in the North. Montrose had beaten the forces sent against him in two brilliant actions at Auldearn and Alford. But his Highlanders, like the troops of Essex and Waller, after a success "got them home" to stow away their booty.

Parliamentary victories in the West. 1645.

Still, if Montrose could not come south, Charles might join him in the North. With this object the king assembled the Yorkshire gentry at Doncaster only to find himself hotly pursued by Colonel Poyntz and the Scottish cavalry under David Leslie, though the latter was soon recalled to Scotland to face Montrose, who had just defeated Baillie at Kilsyth. Any hope of getting to Scotland was spoiled by the wariness of Poyntz, and the king was again obliged to make for Oxford.

The king's last hope.

His marches during these months are well described by Clarendon as "perpetual motion". Leaving Oxford on August 30 he managed to relieve Hereford from the Scots, but his recruiting ground was now worked out, and no forces were available for the relief of Bristol, which Fairfax was now besieging. Again the fugitive king wandered aimlessly northwards, only to see his troops defeated by his pursuer near Chester, on Rowton Heath (Sept. 24). From Newark, he might still reach Montrose. But that brilliant adventurer had just been beaten and ruined, after a year of unprecedented victory, by David Leslie at the surprise of Philiphaugh. Bristol was stormed and surrendered on September 10 by Rupert, who had no liking for a failing cause. When Charles, beaten and low-spirited, once more reached Oxford in October, his position in the Midlands had become untenable owing to the activity of the Parliamentary generals. The next few months were occupied by Cromwell and Fairfax in the complete subjugation of the West. Hopton made a gallant stand, but all was lost early in 1646. Chester had surrendered, Newark was invested by the Scots, and South Wales was all but lost. *A Royal fugitive.*

Such hope as the king now had rested on a treaty with the Scots army. This was possible owing to the disgust of the Northerners at the failure of their hopes for the conversion of England to Presbyterianism, and at the complete success of the Independents in the army of Cromwell and Fairfax. French diplomacy was used to create a superficial agreement between Charles and the Scots, consisting of a verbal treaty in which neither party said what they meant. The result was that the king left Oxford in May, 1646, to take refuge in the Scots camp outside Newark. With the capitulation of Oxford on June 24 the civil war was ended. The Scottish forces retired to Newcastle with the king practically a prisoner in their camp. His position was the result of a resolve to try and get the help of their swords without giving them what they required in return, namely, a definite pledge for Presbyterianism in England. *Flight of the king. May 1646.*

They never intended to take less, and he never meant to grant as much.

In fact, the situation had now changed. Intrigue took the place of war. There were three clear parties: first, the Scots, anxious to make England Presbyterian; secondly, the army of the Parliament flushed with victory, and hating the Scots as much as the Scots hated bishops; lastly, the English Parliament itself, where there were many moderate men in favour of a compromise, and as yet a decided majority for Presbyterianism. Charles's object for the next few years was to play with these three forces in order to secure his own ends, while each party was willing to treat with him, also for its own ends. This explains the constant attempts of the various parties to secure the king's person and so gain his ear.

Altered character of the situation.

The Scots, who held the prize, now combined with Parliament to offer the so-called "Newcastle Propositions". The Parliament was perfectly aware of the Scots' intrigue, in spite of their audacious denial of all knowledge of the king's intended journey to their camp. Yet, fearing the Independents, the majority at Westminster concurred in pressing the treaty, by which Charles was asked to take the Covenant, abolish Episcopacy, and resign the control of militia to Parliament for twenty years. The king's attitude was disappointing. Instead of refusing manfully, he spoke of discussion. The Queen, wiser in her generation, wished him to yield, with the hope of getting back his power gradually. Finally he suggested a compromise, which was refused, and the Scots decided to leave England. Their arrears were paid by Parliament, and the king was handed over to English commissioners, who took him to Holmby House, in Northamptonshire, February, 1647.

Newcastle Propositions. July, 1646.

He at once renewed his negotiations with the English Presbyterians, who were more moderate than the Scots. Their main wish was to get rid of the army, and they were now proposing to send some regiments to Ireland,

and disband others. This led to a most important movement, for the army had long been growing into a political force, and at once organized itself to resist extinction at the hands of a Presbyterian Parliament. Each troop elected a representative, and these chose two "Agitators" for each regiment. {*Parliament versus Army.*} The army was disgusted at the discovery that Parliament was not only scheming to dissolve it, but also concocting an arrangement with the king in the Presbyterian interest. And so Cromwell and the officers, who had not yet sided with the army against Parliament, contrived to arrange the seizure of Charles by Cornet Joyce. He was taken to Newmarket, and there kept up the feud between his enemies by complaining to Parliament of his unlawful seizure by the army. The two forces, military and civil, were now at open strife. The Commons were known to be relying on the London trained-bands, and the army promptly issued its famous manifesto, in which the leaders declared they would march on the city to satisfy their "just demands". The trained-bands were called out, but the army shrank from bloodshed, and the manifesto, on being handed to Parliament, was found to contain a demand for a dissolution, and short Parliaments, in which we can trace the idea of sovereignty of the people. Another peremptory request was for the expulsion of eleven Presbyterian members who had been instrumental in the late negotiations with the king. These prudently fled, but the Commons resolved that the army should not come within 25 miles of London. The flight of the leading Presbyterians made Parliament more inclined to come to terms with the army, but the city was still in favour of accepting a compromise with Charles, and many of the Independent members took refuge from mob violence in the army.

This gave Fairfax an excuse for marching on London, which he did in August, 1647, to restore these members. Meanwhile Cromwell and Fairfax had themselves been endeavouring to come to some terms with the king. But the extreme democratic party {*The march on London.*}

ORIGIN OF THE SECOND CIVIL WAR.

in the army, led by the "Agitators", was for a more complete change, including manhood suffrage and avowed popular sovereignty. Thus the king had a threefold choice, to side with the moderate Presbyterians, to accept the moderate army proposals, or to succumb to the thorough-paced democracy of the "levelling" party.

At first he refused to accept any overtures from the Independents, but subsequently he endeavoured to keep his foes divided by telling Parliament that he preferred the army proposals, and wished to consider them. The army was now thoroughly divided, and the influence of the extreme party was sufficient to raise a storm against Cromwell, who was spoken of as "Judas". A mutiny occurred and was suppressed by the leaders, but it was becoming clear that the Agitators must be reckoned with. They were already speaking of justice on the "man of blood", and Charles began to fear for his safety. In November, 1647, he escaped to the Isle of Wight, still putting his main trust in increasing the conflicts of his enemies. His rejection, however, of the "Four Bills", in which he was asked to give security for Parliament's independence and control over the Militia, at last induced the army and Parliament to forget their differences and combine against him. The vote for discontinuing further "Addresses" to the king was passed in January, 1648.

A split in the army.

It was now clear to Cromwell that no hope remained of coming to terms with Charles. But how to arrange any future agreement between army fanatics, moderate Republicans, and Independents was not so clear.

Difficulties of the army leaders.

For Charles one card remained to play. The Scots had not ceased to ply him with promises, and he now signed an agreement, known as the "Engagement", by which the Scots pledged themselves to restore him to power in return for concessions to Presbyterianism in England. This last proof of duplicity led to the Second Civil War, which broke out at once.

Charles turns to the Scots. Dec. 26, 1647.

The English rising came first; the scattered survivors of the Royalist party took arms on all sides, but they were badly organized, and there was little difficulty in repressing them. Cromwell had a campaign in South Wales, and Fairfax crushed risings at Maidstone and Colchester. The Prince of Wales, to whom a portion of the fleet had turned, threatened the capital, but was compelled to retire for lack of provisions. Somewhat strangely, no enthusiasm was called forth in London, and the city shut its gates on the Royalist forces. *Second civil war. 1648.*

The Scots gave more trouble. Their kingdom was divided into two parties: the extreme Presbyterians under Argyle would have no hand in the rising unless Charles took the Covenant and forswore Bishops and Prayerbook. The more moderate party, with whom the majority of the nobility sided, were opposed to all extreme clericalism, and were willing to fight on Charles's moderate promises. Unfortunately their leader was the incapable Hamilton. Though only partially supported he advanced into England in July. There he was soon to meet Cromwell, who had done his work in Wales and was ready to oppose the Northern host. The Scottish forces were surprised before they could join the English royalists in North Wales. Their English contingent was caught and conquered at Preston (August 17, 1648). The Scottish army decamped towards the South, and Cromwell followed in pursuit through Wigan, taking 10,000 prisoners, some of whom were sent home, while others were sent as slaves to the West Indies. Hamilton capitulated, and the campaign was over.

When the war was finished there was a marked change. The party of moderate Presbyterianism in London had again the upper hand, and was able to send terms to Charles at Newport. But the king only replied by offering a very trifling part of what was asked. In the army, however, there was a much stronger feeling that negotiation must cease and justice begin. He who had caused the second war must be punished now that it was safely ended. Cromwell *Result of the war in England.*

had written from Preston about "destroying those who trouble the land". After sending an ultimatum to the king at Newport on Nov. 16, the Army Council asked for Parliament's concurrence in their "Remonstrance", in which the establishment of democracy and the trial of the king were urged. This was neglected by the Parliament, and the army was exasperated into declaring that Parliament had broken its trust and it was the duty of the army to put a stop to such proceedings. "Pride's Purge", the ejection of the obstinate members by Col. Pride on December 6, left Parliament a tool in the hands of the army. Charles had already been seized by command of the officers and conveyed to Hurst Castle on the Hampshire coast: there was now no further question about bringing him to London for trial. The Commons passed an Ordinance for trying the king on January 1, 1649, and when the Lords refused it the Lower House further declared that as the people are the real source of power the House of Commons might make laws alone. A High Court of Justice was then nominated, but less than half of those originally nominated to it sat to try the king in Westminster Hall.

Legally there was no justification for such a course, as no process can issue against the sovereign. The justification must be sought in moral and political grounds. For us it is enough to note that the prisoner was charged with carrying on "a wicked and tyrannical power, according to his own will", instead of that "limited authority" with which he was intrusted by the nation and laws. Thus was raised in its greatest and most terrible form the question of sovereignty which had already caused so much bloodshed. But thus it found no satisfactory answer. The king's reply, completely convincing according to the old constitution, and the letter of the law, was a restatement of his superiority to law and a criticism of the illegality and partisan character of the court. He was condemned, and beheaded at Whitehall on January 30, 1649, meeting his fate with a dignity and resignation which moved the

Trial and death of the king.

hearts even of his enemies. In the compassion which was felt for his bloody end it was forgotten by most men that he had brought his fate on himself, by his persistent machinations against his captors and his reckless stirring up of the Second Civil War. If he had kept quiet in his captivity he would never have come to the scaffold.

CHAPTER VI.

THE COMMONWEALTH. 1649—1660.

During the next ten years England was practically without a Constitution. One strong man, with a military force behind him, gained the power and kept order amid ever-increasing difficulties. Crom- well aimed at a settlement which should establish peace, toleration, order, and commerce; but he failed to secure them more than temporarily, even by the sword. The reason is not far to seek. As England then was, the task was impossible. It was a political chaos. The nation was split into two hostile camps, and these again into many sections and shades of religious and political opinion. A constable to keep the peace till the ground-works of law and order should be relaid was required. Cromwell achieved this and no more, in spite of brilliant foreign policy and firm suppression of disorder. He never gained the heart of the nation. He would succumb to no party, and no party was willing to sink its own opinions in order to secure the benefits which he was able to confer upon the country. He found and brought no unity. *Character of the Period.*

The Army and the "Rump" (as the sixty Independent members who formed the remnant of the purged Parliament were named) were now supreme. But this supremacy was not likely to produce a peaceful settlement. The Army leaders were not unwilling to work with the mutilated assembly, but the "Agitators" and their programme had still to be reckoned *A Provisional government. 1649.*

with. A scheme brought before Parliament on January 20, entitled "The Agreement of the People", explained their views in favour of a complete democracy. Frequent Parliaments, truly representing the "people", should carry out the national will. But the programme of these Extremists was not adopted. After Kingship and the House of Lords had been abolished, a Council of State was appointed in February, with authority from Parliament to carry on the entire government of the country. There was much talk of the responsibility of this council to Parliament, and of the future free and equally distributed representation of the people; but in talk it stopped. The discontent which the "Levellers" thereon manifested was pitilessly crushed by Cromwell, and a rising of the more hot-headed spirits led to no result but the discredit of their cause.

There was thus a provisional government with everything to settle. But for the present the Republic had to make good its position against a threefold opposition. In Ireland there had existed for eight years a formidable rebellion. If partly religious (for the Catholics of English blood were not given any toleration), it was still more national. The Irish Romanists were demanding, as always, supremacy and separation from England. Hence came the failure of the loyal and high-hearted Ormond to combine the èlements of the rising into a Royalist movement. In the autumn of 1649 Cromwell came over and sacked the towns of Drogheda and Wexford, massacring their garrisons with pitiless severity. His allegation was that slaughter, after due warning, would end opposition, and so be merciful. The struggle speedily showed its true character to be one of race: the English Catholics deserted Ormond and Royalism was crushed. The subjugation of Ireland went on under Ireton; English colonists were introduced and the natives driven behind the line of the Shannon. Cromwell was next called to Scotland, where more work awaited him. After Hamilton's defeat the extreme Presbyterian party was in

Threefold Royalist opposition.

In Ireland.

In Scotland.

power. But they had no wish to see England a Republic with Independency triumphant. Nor had they any sympathy with the execution of the king. They still hoped to obtain from the Prince of Wales the concessions which they had failed to wring from his father at Newcastle. Charles II. had been proclaimed in Edinburgh on his father's execution, but did not go to Scotland until after the failure of the Irish rising. He swallowed the Covenant graciously enough, and the Scottish rising became a fact. In a skilful campaign, which ended with the decisive victory of Dunbar (September 3, 1650), Cromwell stifled once more the hopes of Presbyterian Royalism. But while he was further settling the country, a strong wave of Royalism rose behind him. Hamilton and Montrose had been executed as traitors to their country and the Covenant, but an army of their adherents marched into England with Charles at their head in August, 1651. Cromwell rapidly followed, and at Worcester, his "Crowning Mercy", routed this force on September 3. Prince Charles escaped to France after a thousand adventures, and the opposition in England was crushed. Only at sea did the Royalists under Prince Rupert succeed in giving the navy of the young Republic considerable work; for Royalist piracy, with centres in Scilly and the Channel Islands, continued to menace the trade of the country for some time.

Thus, with a threefold victory at home the new government opened its career. It was not long before foreign affairs called for action. Jealousy of Dutch commercial enterprise led to the passing of the "Navigation Act" in 1651. This aimed at securing for English ships and English capital the lucrative carrying-trade by which the Dutch made large profits out of England's commerce. Henceforth no ship was to land goods in English ports unless she were English made and manned, or belonged to the country whose products she was bringing over. This was to apply the economic doctrine of "protection" to the creation of a merchant navy. The Dutch were naturally angry, and a collision occurred between the English admiral Blake and the celebrated Van Tromp, which led to a declaration of war in July, 1652. The English navy was ably organized, and there was frequent and victorious fighting in the Channel.

But in spite of this successful outset the new government was experiencing grave troubles at home. The party of progress and reform in the army, though baulked of its dearest aims, did not cease to advocate changes; and the old feud between Army and Parliament was always threatening to break out. Cromwell and his council of officers were willing to see some reforms carried out, while the "Rump" did not hesitate to claim the full sovereignty of the unmutilated Parliament. It was not to be expected that such antagonistic principles would long work in harmony. When in November, 1651, the "Rump" consented to dissolve itself, but not till three years should have passed, the Army grew wondrous impatient. The introduction in the spring of 1653 of a bill for making the "Rump" a perpetual Parliament, with a veto on future elections, brought matters to a crisis. The officers were "necessitated, though with much reluctancy, to put an end to this Parliament". Everyone knows how Cromwell entered the House at the head of his musketeers, forcibly evicted the recalcitrant members, and bade his myrmidons "remove that bauble", the Speaker's mace. The Army, though as usual disclaiming any desire to interfere with civil affairs, had once more interfered. This was considered by the Council of State a menace to all government, and its members forthwith dissolved their body. The Lord-general and his officers now stood alone, and England was without a government. The appointment of a fresh Council of State, in which the officers and their chief placed a large majority of their own body, was only a temporary expedient. To Cromwell it seemed that England could be kept in order by the sword, aided by a few local and central officials who would continue to act as if Parliament were sitting. But there were many opponents watching Cromwell. The

Renewed quarrels of Parliament and Army.

Cromwell dissolves the "Rump".

"Saints", as the extreme Independents were called, were claiming to rule the earth. The true Republicans, who thought Saints should be modest and wait till the kingdom was given them, were anxious for a settled free government by and for the people —"government by consent", as they called it. To neither of these views could Cromwell subscribe: his answer was complete. "Where," he asked, "shall we find the consent? Amongst the Prelatical, Presbyterian, Independent, Anabaptist, or Levelling parties?" This is the key to his position. A free Parliament he would not allow, for a free Parliament meant Royalty, and the nation finally refused to take anything less.

<small>The new Constitutional Problem.</small>

For the moment, however, he thought it wise to allow the "Saints" to try their hand. A body of nominees, mainly chosen by the Independent ministers, was summoned, to the number of 144. To them Cromwell committed the affairs of the kingdom. They began to reform and abolish with vigour, and finally, in their zeal, threatened to upset the institution of private property by attacking tithes and patronage. Their assembly, which is known as "Barebones Parliament", because one of its prominent members bore that extraordinary name, resigned its power in December, 1653.

<small>First attempt to solve it.</small>

The army leaders under Lambert now proposed to make Cromwell "Lord Protector", with a council and a Parliament in due form. The Proposal was drawn up in the "Instrument of Government". It was a new kind of constitution, for all the powers of Protector and Parliament were carefully defined and separated, no alteration in their respective powers being allowed. The liberty of the Commons was preserved by its being made impossible for the Protector to dissolve them till they should have sat five months. Here then was the barrier against party violence, and to this barrier Cromwell looked to save the kingdom.

<small>The "Instrument", December 16, 1653.</small>

With a settled form of government all might go well, and in foreign affairs the outlook was promising. The Dutch had been beaten and

<small>Peace with Holland. 1654.</small>

brought to terms, and now bowed before English commercial supremacy. Cromwell had allied himself closely with Sweden in order to keep open the Baltic trade against the monopolizing spirit of Danes and Dutch, and it was this alliance which had brought the latter to terms.

The test of the new government would be a Parliament, and this met in September, 1654. Scotland and Ireland were for the first time represented at Westminster, and a rational rearrangement of the constituencies, foreshadowing in many points the famous Reform Bill of 1832, had been carried out. But Cromwell's plan met with little respect. His opponents in the new Parliament discussed the very foundation of the whole, "government in the hands of a single person and Parliament". The Protector thereupon declared that they were not to criticise any "fundamental" part of the new scheme, and turned out of Parliament those who persisted in doing so. Yet the remainder proved so obstinate that a dissolution occurred after the legal five months stipulated in the "Instrument". The unpopularity in which this *coup d'état* involved the Protector caused the Royalists to attempt a rising in Wiltshire under Penruddock. It was easily suppressed, but the need of strengthening the central authority in the country districts led to a new device. England divided into eleven provinces, over which as officers were placed. These "Major-generals" we organize the local militia, and to use it for police purposes. This temporarily abrogated the system of local government established by the Tudors. The institutions of the country were in abeyance, taxes were imposed illegally, and men were arbitrarily imprisoned. Republicans and Independents complained of these "pashas" and their high-handed doings. Yet much was done which made in the Protector's favour. Men nominated to livings were carefully supervised by a board of "Triers". Jews were allowed to return to England for the first time since 1290. The legal system was reformed and simplified. Yet discontent increased.

Parliament upsets the scheme.

When a new parliament assembled in September, 1656, foreign politics were for the moment in the ascendant. The two great powers of France and Spain were now face to face on the conclusion of the Thirty Years War; each was anxious for the alliance of England. Cromwell chose France. This secured the expulsion of Prince Charles from French soil, and was more likely to satisfy glowing Protestantism than any dealings with Spain. Philip IV. was the champion of Catholicism, and, moreover, claimed a complete monopoly of the West Indian trade. English enterprise found vent in a successful attack on the rich isle of Jamaica, and war was declared against Spain in February, 1656. It was not long before France actively joined in the war, and Cromwell was able to secure from her the restoration of the Protestants of the Waldensian Valleys, whom the Duke of Savoy had been persecuting. Dunkirk was taken for England before the Protector's death.

France or Spain?

The new Parliament had been carefully packed. The "Instrument" had given the Protector's Council the power to reject members who were considered "disabled to be elected". Nearly 100 Republicans and Presbyterians having been thus excluded, the remainder proceeded to offer Cromwell the title of king under a new documentary constitution. This "Humble Petition and Advice" gave more freedom and power to Parliament, though it still remained powerless to touch any of the "fundamentals". A house of Peers was also to be created. Cromwell, after much debate, refused to take the kingship, but accepted the rest of the new constitution.

The "Petition and Advice", 1657.

When Parliament met again in January, 1658, the members before excluded were allowed to take their seats, as no power of scrutiny had been put in the hands of the government by the "Petition and Advice". Their objection to the new constitution, and to the "other house", as they called Cromwell's Peers, made it impossible for the Protector to keep them in session without altering his views. He

Again the plan fails.

expected his Parliament to be loyal to a constitution which many of them had had no hand in framing: as this was impossible, he dissolved them. It was useless for him to beg for unity in the face of the dangers which from time to time threatened the Republic. They would not listen.

Thus he who for years had kept England safe, prosperous, and respected, had settled nothing. His death, which occurred in September, 1658, left the problem of government to be faced by men infinitely less able than himself. <small>Death of the Protector.</small>

The late Lord Protector's rule had satisfied no party, though it had curbed all: and now the strife was going to break out again. His son Richard, who succeeded by virtue of the provisions of the "Petition and Advice", was both by taste and education a mere country gentleman. <small>Richard's short Protectorate.</small> He had neither the power nor the wish to take up the task which lay before him, and his speedy fall made way for absolute anarchy. Cromwell had foreseen this; but when he had named the many parties whose existence made free government impossible, he had omitted to speak of one— the party which would restore the king in order to secure order and peace.

On Richard's accession, the military officers under Lambert, Fleetwood, and others at once began to demand for the army a leader independent of the civil government. <small>Quarrel with the Army.</small> Oliver had been both General and Protector, but Richard hardly knew a pike from a musket. To resist this movement the new Protector summoned a Parliament, in which he had a majority against the "Wallingford House" party, as the officers were named. His Protectorate was recognized, and the army, finding that they were outvoted in Parliament, demanded a dissolution. Richard, fearing an outbreak of civil war, took the only sensible course and abdicated, on the 22d of April, 1659.

The party of Lambert, with whom the Republican foes of the Protectorate were allied, was now supreme. But it contained a strong leaven of "Levellers" and other extremists. A fresh element of discord was added when its leaders resolved to restore the "Rump" Parliament, which had been driven from Westminster by Oliver.

<small>The army restores the "Rump", May, 1659.</small>

The tottering fabric of the Republic now consisted of this caricature of a Parliament—it consisted of only 40 members,—a few self-seeking soldier leaders, and an army which was daily becoming more unpopular owing to its connection with the Levelling programmes. The wildest discord was rife between the civil and military elements. Parliament claimed supremacy, while the Army, fresh from Lambert's victory over some Royalists in Cheshire, did not care to conceal its claim to complete independence. Finally, in October, 1659, relying on the adherence of Monk, who was commanding in Scotland, the "Rump" took the daring step of depriving of their commissions Lambert and those of his friends who had encouraged petitions in favour of the independence of the Army. The irate officers replied by driving the "Rump" a second time from Westminster.

<small>And quarrels ensue.</small>

George Monk, from his post beyond the Tweed, was grimly watching the dance at Westminster. Nominally a Presbyterian, certainly loathing the whole race of Sectaries and Levellers, he saw in Lambert's triumph nothing but danger for the future. When it was announced that he was preparing to march into England, the very rumour of his opposition sufficed to overthrow the military government in London; and while Lambert marched northward to confront Monk, the "Rump" returned uninvited to Westminster. The fleet held to the civil power, the sailors petitioned for a free and full Parliament, and such leaders of the Army as could be safely touched were banished.

<small>Intervention of Monk.</small>

Monk started from Scotland on New-year's Day, 1660. In London, where he was at once completely master of affairs, he restored the Presbyterian members expelled by Colonel Pride twelve years before, and declared for a free Parliament. The Royalist Pres-

<small>His march to London.</small>

byterian members were now in a majority. Writs were issued for a free "Convention", and the Long Parliament at last consented of its own free will to dissolve itself (March, 1660). The new convention Parliament contained a large majority for the moderates. On all sides was heard the cry for the restoration of the old order. Charles was in Holland, and issued from Breda, at Monk's suggestion, his famous "Declaration". It promised amnesty, toleration, and a general settlement of the kingdom in accordance with the decisions of Parliament. This was considered sufficient. The more prudent Presbyterians wished for some clearer understanding with the prince, but the nation would not wait. The reaction was in full flow. The first act of the Convention was to invite Charles to return, and to resolve that government in England was vested in King, Lords, and Commons. The *Naseby*, rechristened for the occasion the *Royal Charles*, brought the king to Dover, and he reached the capital on May 29 amid universal rejoicings. *[The King's Return.]*

CHAPTER VII.

CHARLES II.: 1660–1685.

Charles, the eldest son of the late monarch, was thus accepted as king, not so much because he had a right to the position, as because the nation could not get on without him. The experience of the last few years was felt to be worse than anything that had gone before. Men of all conditions now rallied to the side of the crown because it was likely to be the champion of a known order of government. Cavaliers and Republicans, Presbyterians and Churchmen made a temporary alliance in the interests of the old constitution. *[Character of the Restoration.]*

The Rebellion had settled hardly anything. The problem of Sovereignty was still without a solution. There should not be a sovereign army or a sovereign presbytery; in that, and that only, men were agreed. The question of Toleration was not answered. The country was just as much split up into parties as before, but the nation as a whole was nervous about *order*, and forgot to be anxious about liberty. One thing alone was tolerably certain as a result of the long struggle. No future king could hope to set himself for any long period against the will of the entire people. If Charles wished to have his own way it must also be the way of the nation, or of a clear majority of the nation. Ship money or forced loans were not likely to recur. If this was the net result of the war it would soon become clear that the king had a fair chance to rule as he pleased, provided he could play off the numerous parties against each other, and keep the fear of civil war well before the eyes of moderate men.

Result of the Rebellion.

Now this is exactly what Charles did. He was a cool-headed selfish man, with admirable manners, and no convictions to trouble him. He was not likely to make a crusade to save bishops, or to save anything. But he liked his own way, not because he felt that he had a duty to do, but because he found it pleasant to be independent. Yet on one point he shared his father's and grandfather's ideas. He believed in the mission of the Stewart family, and would put up even with personal inconvenience rather than repudiate the Divine hereditary right. Fortunately for him, he possessed, along with this view, the inestimable gift of tact, in which his family was generally so conspicuously wanting. He knew as well as anybody that he could not withstand the whole nation. As he himself put it, he did not wish "to go on his travels again".

Character of Charles.

Hence the whole reign became a struggle, in which the king, however much he might offend one party, was never without a party to side with him. The reason of this is to be looked for in the old religious parties—which now take three forms—Churchmen, Protestant Dissenters of all sorts, and Roman

Character of the Reign.

ANALYSIS OF THE REIGN. 71

Catholics. Here were sufficient sources of discord on a vital question; a fourth element was soon added—the King of France. Charles was not proud, and if his parliament or his opposition proved troublesome he would apply for money and advice to Louis XIV. That prince generally found it worth his while to supply both.

There are five well-marked periods into which the twenty-five years of this reign may be divided. The first lasted only about a year, and witnessed the attempt of the Convention Parliament to settle the outstanding questions of religion and politics on a moderate basis. Its place was taken by the "Cavalier" Parliament, which set to work to strengthen the revived monarchy, re-establish the Anglican Church, and persecute all other creeds. This was during the full tide of reaction against the ideals of Puritanism. The second period (1662–1672) finds this Parliament gradually losing confidence in the king, whose schemes of toleration it hated, and whose minister it impeached. The king and his secret councillors now trafficked with Louis, and there gradually appeared a fair possibility of a complete reaction against the restored monarchy. Two parties were forming; one that of the Parliament, whose religious policy had been outraged, another the popular party, which hated the foreign intrigues and the persecuting statutes to which the king had assented. The third period (1672–1679) was one in which this twofold opposition failed to combine against the crown, and Charles was able to play off his opponents one against the other. In the fourth period (1679–1681) a great opposition, the beginning of the future Whig party, was organized, and the attempt was made to oust the Duke of York, an avowed Papist, from the succession to the crown. This question divided the nation, and the popular party, in the hands of immoderate men, wrecked its own cause. The last period (1681–1685) found the king secure and triumphant, free from Parliament, and from his other enemies, who had roused the fears of the nation, and hurried all those who cared more for order than for liberty into the royal camp.

Periods of the Reign.

The Convention, which had no strict claim to the name of Parliament since it was not summoned by royal writ, had a tremendous problem to deal with. After such a time of religious and political discord it was no easy task to set things in order.

The Restoration Settlement, 1660.

Some revenge upon the regicides was to be expected, and thirteen of the most prominent were put to death. A bill of Indemnity, covering the whole period from 1637 to 1660, secured other men from punishment. The House of Lords was restored, and the bishops regained their seats. The army was disbanded, the royal income fixed at £1,200,000 per annum, and the crown lands restored. But the Cavaliers, who had been obliged to sell their lands, were not reinstated if they had in any way recognized the usurping government. The religious question was far more difficult. The king had been both a Covenanter and a Roman Catholic in his time, and it now suited him to pose as an Anglican. The Convention represented that combination of Churchmen and Presbyterians which had brought back the king. They restored the clergy who had been ejected from livings by the Puritans, but did not disturb men who had been rightly inducted by the patrons, and thus left many Presbyterians and Independents in possession of livings. The only arrangement which could make this system work well would have been a scheme of "comprehension", which is the term used for the adaptation of the Church to suit the views of the more moderate Dissenters. The king wished to carry this out, but as he included toleration for Independents and Roman Catholics, it was not likely that the Churchmen and Presbyterians would agree to it.

In December, 1660, this famous Assembly was dissolved, and an intensely strong Anglican and Cavalier spirit animated the new Parliament. It condemned the claims of the Long Parliament to regulate the militia, and declared that force to be entirely in the hands of the crown. The religious reaction was complete; and after the failure of a confer-

The "Cavalier" Parliament, 1661-1679.

ence at the Savoy Palace, in which Churchmen and Presbyterians made an ineffectual attempt to bridge over their differences, the true character of the change was shown. Parliament passed the Corporation Act (1661), by which all members of town corporations were compelled to renounce the Covenant, repudiate the right of people to resist the crown, and receive the Sacrament as Churchmen. The king was obliged to accept this policy as he was in need of money, and Parliament cared more for their church than even for their king. In May, 1662, the Presbyterians who still held livings were confronted by the "Act of Uniformity", which compelled all beneficed clergy to accept the Prayer Book, and two thousand ministers quitted their posts rather than submit. It was not unnatural that Churchmen should think it necessary that men who held benefices should be ordained by bishops and believe in the legal church. But they had shown a persecuting spirit in forcing town officers to believe as they did, and were soon to cruelly persecute those who had been removed from office in the Church. The Cavaliers had now struck a blow at their enemies in town and parish, and carried the king with them. They shortly afterwards took vengeance on Sir Harry Vane, the hero of the scene in the House of Commons when Strafford's famous words in the Council were produced. He, with Lambert, was tried for treason, on the ground that Charles II. was legally king during the period of Cromwell's government. Vane was executed on this flimsy argument. The next period raises the question how far Charles could be dragged along by this party.

The chief minister was now the Earl of Clarendon, who, as Sir Edward Hyde, had been one of Charles the First's most trusted advisers. He was strongly opposed to Toleration, and wished the Church to keep her supremacy. Indeed, the persecuting statutes of this period have been named the "Clarendon Code". Charles did not like the domination of Clarendon any better than the supremacy of Parliament, but, for a time, all went well. The king was married (1662) to a

Clarendon's Administration, 1660-1667.

Portuguese princess, Catharine of Braganza. This alliance naturally brought the English government into line with France, for Louis was supporting Portugal in the maintenance of her independence against Spain. The sale of Dunkirk to the French king bound this friendship closer, and pleased Charles, who saw in the purchase-money a means of independence. But there was no harmony, for the king was already talking of using his inherent power of dispensing[1] with laws in order to lighten the burdens upon Roman Catholics and Protestant Dissenters. Parliament and the Chancellor Clarendon agreed in resisting this royal attempt to undermine their policy.

A war with Holland temporarily united king and Parliament. The Dutch were still our commercial rivals on the sea and our colonial opponents in the Indies. In the days of King James English Puritan colonists had sailed to the shores of North America, and the descendants of these famous "Pilgrim Fathers" had now established a great group of colonies east of the Hudson river. This settlement was known as New England. Lower down the coast, Virginia, the oldest of the English settlements abroad, had grown into a prosperous slave-owning country. Between these two settlements was a district colonized by the Dutch, and hence constant quarrels arose. Charles was also angry with Holland on his own account. His sister Mary had married the Prince of Orange, who died young. On his decease the Dutch refused to continue his son William III. in his father's office of Stadtholder. A great statesman, named de Witt, now guided Dutch politics, under the title of Grand Pensionary, and the young William of Orange, Charles's nephew, the future King of England, was kept out of the chief-magistracy which his ancestors had held for three generations.

The Dutch war, 1665-1667.

The war broke out in 1665, and was hotly waged at sea. The King of France, for the moment, joined the Dutch against England. His policy was a deep and clever one.

---

[1] Dispensing power means the ancient Royal right to pardon the breach of an Act: suspending power is a claim to declare the Act or Acts to be no longer in force.

The real object which he had in view was the extension of France to the Rhine, and the gradual absorption of the decaying Spanish empire. For these two objects he strove until his death. All the lands between the French border and the Rhine—the Spanish Netherlands (Belgium), Luxembourg, Lorraine, the county of Burgundy, and Alsace—were meant to be attacked in turn. Louis' wife was the sister of King Charles II. of Spain, a sickly boy, who, it was hoped, would soon die. His vast inheritance might then fall to the French king, in spite of his renunciation in the Treaty of the Pyrenees of all future rights which should accrue through his wife. All this was plainly opposed to Dutch interests, for the Dutch were bound to resent the approach of so powerful a monarch to their frontiers.[1] But Louis was, for the present, pledged by treaty to assist them, and did not wish to show his hand.

Louis XIV. and his schemes.

When Louis declared war (1666) the English government was extending its policy of persecution, being alarmed lest the Dissenters should side with the Dutch. Thus the cruel Conventicle Act imposed in 1664 severe penalties against those who should worship in any way other than that prescribed by the Act of Uniformity; and in 1665 the Dissenting ministers were further forbidden by the Five Mile Act to approach within five miles of any corporate town, and so debarred from earning a livelihood by teaching. The great Plague was raging in London, and a few months later the great Fire destroyed a large part of the city. Thus England was prepared by her disunion and disaster rather for peace than for war. The Dutch also became alive to the dangers with which they were threatened by Louis' schemes. Thus negotiations were opened between the two principals. In order to hasten the English into peace de Witt sent his vessels into the Thames and Medway, and "the roar of foreign guns was heard for the first and last time by the citizens of London". In the end England secured the Dutch colonies

English difficulties, 1665-1667.

Peace of Breda, July, 1667.

[1] See map p. 105.

between New England and Virginia, while the Dutch kept their hold on the Spice Islands of the East Indies.

For some time discontent had been growing both in and out of Parliament; there were grave scandals as to the management of public money voted for the War; there were rumours that the king had a design to ally himself with France and to govern without a Parliament by means of armed force; small as the standing army was, since all but a few regiments had been disbanded in 1660, it was not unnaturally considered a menace to freedom; the sale of Dunkirk was thought almost as great a national disgrace as the burning of English shipping by the Dutch in the Medway. All ills were ascribed to the minister. Charles was not inclined to exert himself to save his father's old friend, for Clarendon did not share his views as to Toleration, or scruple to show contempt for the king's immoral life. He was impeached and banished.

Fall of Clarendon, August, 1667.

The next administration is known in history as the "Cabal", because the names of the men who were chiefly consulted by the king during the next few years were found to spell Cabal[1] by their initial letters. They were Clifford and Arlington, who were Roman Catholics; Buckingham, the son of James I.'s favourite; Anthony Ashley, afterwards Earl of Shaftesbury; and Lauderdale, who was governing Scotland in the Episcopal interest and persecuting the Covenanters, who, after the execution of their leader Argyle at the Restoration, continued to be an oppressed and discredited party until the end of the century. These five men were widely different in their ideas, and had but one common object—a broader view in church matters than was prevalent in Parliament.

The "Cabal", 1667-1673.

Louis was alarming the Dutch by his successes in the Spanish Netherlands, which he was now claiming by right of his wife. Englishmen were hostile to the advance of the great Catholic monarch, and an alliance was made by England, Holland, and Sweden to force him to desist.

[1] Cabal = Cabala, secret knowledge of the occult sort.

He gave way for the time, and restored the county of Burgundy, though he kept several recently acquired fortresses in the Netherlands. But Charles had never cared for the popular policy of the Triple Alliance, and soon entered into a secret negotiation with the French king. Louis was anxious to crush the Dutch, who were bound to be the opponents of his grasping frontier policy, and was most anxious to bind Charles and the English to neutrality if not to co-operation. Parliament was opposed to Louis, and therefore Charles could not join him unless he obtained money for doing so, since such an alliance was bound to alienate his subjects. Here at last was a chance to get free from the leading strings in which the "Cavalier Parliament" had kept him, and the king seized it. By the secret Treaty of Dover, known only to Clifford and Arlington, Charles agreed to help Louis against the Dutch, and to declare himself a Roman Catholic for a round sum of £200,000 a year. This treaty was nearly as ridiculous as it was disgraceful. That the English would ever allow themselves to be led back to Popery by their king ought by this time to have been clear even to a Stewart. *Triple Alliance and Treaty of Dover, 1668-1670.*

The real policy of the Cabal was shown when in 1672 the king issued his famous Declaration of Indulgence. The Parliament, which had already shown itself more zealous for the church than for the crown, was not sitting at the moment; and the king's supposed power to suspend ecclesiastical laws was used to grant freedom from the stringent penal laws to both Nonconformists and Roman Catholics. The leader of this policy was Ashley, who had just been made Earl of Shaftesbury and Lord Chancellor. *The Indulgence.*

When Parliament met in 1673, after a long prorogation, the Declaration of Indulgence was before their eyes, though the treaty with Louis was still a secret. War had just been declared against Holland, and men who knew nothing of the secret plot were not sorry to punish Holland for her attack on English ships *Opposition increases.*

in 1667. The third period of the reign opens with this session, in which the king soon found himself opposed to two parties: the Cavaliers, who resented the Declaration, and the moderate men, who began to fear that the Declaration was only part of the French alliance, and tended to Roman Catholicism and arbitrary government rather than to the relief of Protestant Dissenters.

At first the Parliament was eager for the war against the Dutch. Shaftesbury, the Lord Chancellor, made his celebrated speech, in which he announced the policy of the French alliance (he knew nothing of the secret treaty) in the words "Delenda est Carthago". Parliament voted large sums, but showed no sign of bowing to the Indulgence scheme. It was not long before its views were more clearly expressed. The king had to withdraw the Declaration, and the Test Act was passed. It declared that all who held any office under the crown must renounce the doctrine of Transubstantiation and receive the Sacrament in the English Church. This was the final blow to the Cabal.

The Test Act, 1673.

Meanwhile Englishmen were becoming alarmed at the successes of Louis. Perhaps some suspicions of the secret treaty were abroad. The war with Holland became unpopular; the fear of Roman Catholicism increased when men reflected that we were at war with a Protestant power in alliance with a Catholic one. Many feared that Charles would use his army to make himself independent, for the Commonwealth was not forgotten; and Shaftesbury, the apostle of toleration, was dismissed. He very soon entered the ranks of the opposition, but not, of course, to act in alliance with the bigoted Churchmen who had passed the Test Act. The various elements of this opposition were not likely to unite, and so the king, at present, had little to fear. Shaftesbury had been willing to use the Royal Prerogative to gain Toleration, and could not therefore complain with Parliament of the Suspending power. The Cavaliers of the Test Act were not likely to join the originators of the Indulgence. But the

A disunited opposition.

opposition to France was too strong to be resisted, and in 1674 Charles cleverly yielded so much, and made peace with Holland. Thus the king had twice yielded his point, in each case on the question of religion, for his alliance with Louis was really a Catholic policy. So disunited were his opponents, however, that he might have been absolute if he had desisted from all religious opposition to Parliament.

There was in 1675 a return to the policy of Clarendon when Sir Thomas Osborne, Earl of Danby, a strong churchman and a friend of royalty, became chief adviser of the crown. But the popularity of this long Parliament was now waning. *Danby, chief minister, 1675.* It had outstayed its welcome. Men were tired of its factious temper, especially when Danby produced a bill to impose on all "placemen[1]" an oath that they would neither resist the crown nor attempt alteration of government in church or state. This, however, he failed to convert into law. The leaders of the Toleration party were anxious for a dissolution, as they hoped for a broader religious feeling in the next Parliament. That the nation was partly of the same opinion may be gathered from the fact that the government thought proper to order the closing of the "coffee-houses", in which men were in the habit of *Feeling against Parliament, 1670.* discussing politics, there being no newspapers to read. Lastly the king of France, who was now obliged to face a general European coalition against his schemes, was most anxious to see the "Cavalier Parliament" dissolved. Their strong anti-French attitude might, he thought, force Charles into a French war as it had already forced him into a Dutch peace. When, after more than a year's prorogation, Parliament reassembled in February, 1677, Louis' anticipations were realized, and a cry for a French war arose. The opposition lords, with Shaftesbury at their head, maintained that a year's prorogation dissolved *ipso facto* a Parliament, since, by the old laws, there must be a meeting every year. This was a mere quibble for

[1] Persons holding office under the crown.

the Triennial Act of 1641, requiring a meeting at least once in three years, was still in force, though its more stringent provisions had been repealed. But the action of these leaders serves to show that there was an opposition to both king and Parliament.

In this situation the shrewd king once more proved his tact. Since Parliament was averse to France he determined to side with them and desert his French alliance. He would thus play off Parliament against the Toleration party, which suspected his Roman Catholic designs. The money which he could no longer obtain from Louis he would be able to get from his subjects, for, his real aim being to strengthen his army in case of future need, money was absolutely necessary. Thus the Toleration party, which could not, like Louis and Parliament, supply money, was isolated. A grand opportunity to persuade a rather incredulous Parliament of his anti-French intentions now presented itself, and the king was not slow to take it. During the Dutch war the Grand Pensionary had been murdered by a mob, and the young Prince of Orange had been restored, at the age of twenty-one, to the Stadtholdership. This Protestant prince, the lifelong enemy of the great French king, was now married, with the approval of Charles, to his cousin Mary, eldest daughter of James, Duke of York, the king's brother. Parliament was greatly pleased at this third marked success. They voted a million, and the astute king was able to add to his army. He soon found, however, that he had only exchanged masters.

The king's change of policy, 1677.

And as for Louis his revenge was easy. There was a growing fear in England that Charles had meant to secure his own independence of Parliament by an army and French help. The French king cleverly stimulated this fear, and took into his pay several of the unscrupulous leaders of the English opposition, while assuring them that he had deserted the cause of their sovereign. The Toleration party, forsaken by Charles, was taken up by Louis!

The opposition and Louis XIV.

This was, indeed, a sufficient complication, and yet Charles added another string to his bow by asking Louis to pay him large sums to enable him to be independent of the Cavalier Parliament. So intricate had the politics of England become that, though king and Parliament were apparently in alliance against France, both were asking money from that power to do its behests. Such a situation could not last. The French king took the opportunity to make peace with Holland at Nimuegen (August, 1678), and obtained his coveted county of Burgundy together with many fortresses in the Netherlands. Parliament was becoming more and more nervous as to the intentions of Charles. The opposition was becoming stronger and clearer, though there was, as yet, no great question on which they could unite. *A complicated situation, 1678.*

At this moment the king's luck deserted him. There arose a cry on which the opposition could appeal to a sensitive nation. The Popish Plot, a tissue of falsehoods weaved around a slender thread of fact, was announced by a depraved villain named Titus Oates. He, and others like him, declared that there was a deep-rooted plot by which Roman Catholics were endeavouring to subvert the freedom of the country, assassinate the king, and restore England to the Papal allegiance. The nation was alarmed. The old fears of the French alliance and the Indulgence had made the way easy for such a panic. Parliament caught the alarm, Papists were hurried to execution on the slenderest evidence, and the opposition leaders, some of whom believed genuinely in the story, fanned the flames. An act to disable Papists from sitting in either house of Parliament was passed. As if to show where the *real* Popish Plot had been, the secret of a letter, written by Danby at the king's bidding, in which the English ambassador was instructed to ask Louis for money, was now made public by Danby's enemies. The old Treaty of Dover was as yet only suspected. The minister was at once impeached. Charles avowed his own orders, and, to screen his too faithful servant, dissolved the Cavalier *The Popish Plot and the Dissolution, 1678.*

Parliament. Louis had, for the moment, the game in his hands, and the opposition had gained a case to lay before the country.

In the fourth period of the reign this case took a definite shape, and led dangerously near to rebellion. James, the king's brother, was heir to the throne, for Charles had no legitimate children. He was a declared Roman Catholic, and had recently married as his second wife the Princess Mary of Modena, who was of the same faith. His first wife was Anne Hyde, daughter of the Chancellor Clarendon, and mother of James's daughters, Mary and Anne, who were afterwards Queens of England. With the Popish Plot filling men's mouths, an army still on foot in spite of Parliamentary demands for its disbandment, and Louis XIV. still successfully creeping up to the Rhine frontier, it was not difficult for the opposition to raise a cry that the Protestant Constitution was in danger. They struck straight at the one idea which Charles cherished more than his ease or his independence—the hereditary right of his family; and demanded security against a Popish successor. Lord William Russell led in the Commons, while Shaftesbury represented the opposition in the Lords. Charles tried to divert attention from James by adopting a Protestant foreign policy, but when Danby pleaded the royal pardon to bar his impeachment another strong case was added to the score of the popular party; for Parliament declared such a pardon to be illegal. At last there was a point which the king would not yield and could not, by shuffling the cards, evade.

New Parliament and strong opposition, March, 1679.

At this critical moment Sir William Temple brought forward his celebrated scheme intended to solve the ever-recurring conflicts between Parliament and the crown. He proposed that the Privy Council should be reconstructed and made a sort of mediator between king and Parliament. It was to consist of thirty members, fifteen royal nominees, and fifteen members of the Legislature. They were to advise the crown, and no step was to be taken without them.

Temple to the rescue, 1679.

A CANDIDATE FOR THE THRONE. 83

Charles adopted this cumbrous plan. Many of his bitterest opponents were made members, Shaftesbury becoming President. The king now hoped to stave off the succession difficulty, and offered extraordinary securities for Protestantism, provided the Duke of York was allowed to succeed in due course. All holders of places of trust, together with the military and naval administration, were to be approved by Parliament, which was to be secured from a dissolution at the time of the king's death.

But the leaders of the Opposition were not to be silenced. They rightly concluded that such safeguards were illusory, for no Parliament can bind its successors; and in May, 1679, the Exclusion Bill, to prevent the succession of James, was produced. *Exclusion Bill, 1679.* The king meant to go to all lengths to prevent this; and therefore, after passing the celebrated Habeas Corpus Act, which secured that the ancient writ to enquire into the cause of imprisonment should not be evaded by legal officers, his third Parliament was dissolved. The Council scheme had completely failed.

The idea of Exclusion involved some plan for a successor other than James. And it is here that Shaftesbury and his party made their greatest mistake. They openly proposed to seat the Duke of *Monmouth's candidature.* Monmouth, one of the many natural sons of the king, upon the throne of England. Monmouth was popular, and had gained some military reputation, having just won a victory over the extreme Covenanters in Scotland at Bothwell Brig, and suppressed a very dangerous rising. There were not wanting agitators who spread a tale of Charles's marriage with Lucy Walters, the young Duke's mother. This the king emphatically denied, and the persistence of the Shaftesbury faction in this plan brought about a split even in the ranks of the Opposition. Lord Halifax, a brilliant and adventurous politician, threw in his lot with the government. He is generally known as the "Trimmer", for he loved to desert the winning side and thus gratify his vanity by rectifying the balance. Russell and others still adhered to Shaftesbury.

Once more a Parliament was elected in October, 1679, but Charles refused to summon it, and for a year the members never assembled. It is during this time that the names Whig and Tory were first given to the two parties. Those who believed in the Popish Plot, and wished to change the succession, were derisively compared to the "Whigamores", or "Whigs", a bitter sect of Scottish Covenanters. Those who adhered to the Court and Divine Right were styled "Tories", a name by which the outlawed banditti of Ireland were known. The Whigs petitioned for a summons of Parliament, while the Tories arranged counter-petitions "abhorring" the idea of altering the succession. Thus the terms "Petitioners" and "Abhorrers" were also used to describe the two factions. Beneath the question of the succession lay the great dispute, which had commenced in the days of the Long Parliament, as to whether the nation was to have a personal king or an official one. For it was practically the same thing to discuss whether a nation may choose a king or must accept a distasteful one because of his pedigree. The Stewart theory of Divine Right trembled in the balance, as that of the Discretionary power of monarchs had in the days of Charles I. and Laud. The two great parties had a different view of the question of Sovereignty, as they had of the question of Toleration.

Whigs and Tories, 1680.

In October, 1680, the Parliament at last met. Charles tried once more to shelve the question by asking for unity in the face of the French king's advances towards the Dutch frontier. But men saw through this, and knew that he probably had another letter about French gold ready for his ministers. Besides, Louis had been careful to keep up the quarrel, for he knew England was a dangerous factor in European politics if it was united. He worked up the fears of arbitrary government, and the Exclusion Bill was passed in the Commons. In the Lords, however, Halifax made a brilliant speech, cutting deeply into the Whig programme. The two Protestant daughters of James, Mary, Princess of Orange, and Anne, were excluded by Shaftesbury's

Rejection of the Bill.

scheme, and the Lords, taught by Halifax, refused to adopt it.

But the Opposition could not now retreat. Already there was a talk in Parliament of Toleration and Comprehension, and the city of London was pledged to the Exclusion Bill. Charles once more dissolved Parliament, and summoned a new one to Oxford, in order to be out of the way of Shaftesbury's "brisk boys", as the mobs he hoped to raise were styled. In March, 1681, this Assembly met in Christ Church Hall. The Whig leaders, fearing lest they might be molested in that home of Royalism, came with armed followers, an unconstitutional blunder to which they largely owed their ruin. The question speedily came to an issue. Charles offered everything; even to make the Prince of Orange Regent during his brother's lifetime, provided the title of king were reserved to the latter, who might be banished from the kingdom. This was clever, for it forced Shaftesbury to rely on the Duke of Monmouth as his candidate. Charles refused point blank to recognize his natural son as heir to the throne. He had split the Opposition by this manœuvre, and knew that he had Louis' gold in reserve, for the latter would not care to see a new government under Monmouth and Shaftesbury pledged to a Protestant policy. Louis only wanted Charles to quarrel with his parliament, and would pay either, or both, so long as they were not on speaking terms. The last Parliament of King Charles was at once dissolved after one week's stormy session.

The last Parliament March, 1681.

The last period of the reign witnesses a great Tory reaction. There was no Parliament. William of Orange came to ask his uncle's help against the French, who were overrunning Alsace, but obtained no assistance. The Cavaliers, who feared their church policy would collapse if Shaftesbury and his party obtained power, now rallied to the king. To prevent the Dissenters from getting a footing in politics they were willing to keep to hereditary succession, just as their ancestors had rallied to Charles, rather than trust the Church

The turn of the tide.

to Pym and the Puritans. The entire moderate party were more alarmed at the menacing attitude of the Whigs than at the royal army which Charles maintained or at the seizure of Strasburg by Louis XIV. Civil war was an evil they never meant to face again. Thus there was for the first time in the reign no need for the king to give way. He had not to choose between abandoning his brother and "starting on his travels", for the majority of the nation, sensitive as they were about Popery, chose for him. James they considered a less evil than civil war.

Thus the conditions enabled the king to change his tactics. Instead of defending hereditary right, which men were now eager to do for him; he was able to attack its assailants. Shaftesbury was accused of treason. The London grand jury, to the delight of the Whigs, threw out the bill. But the men who now advised Charles—Sunderland, Lawrence Hyde, and Halifax—were determined to crush their opponents. London, which, by adhering to Parliament, had ruined Charles I., and had so recently proved itself a stronghold of the Whigs, saw its gates thrown down and its privileges attacked. On various trifling pretexts the ancient charter of the capital city was confiscated, and was only renewed upon conditions which ensured a subservient corporation. A similar fate was meted out to other towns, and the great centres of Dissent and Whiggery were thus rendered harmless. Meanwhile Shaftesbury's ill-advised design to appeal to arms on the question of the Succession completed the ruin of the already discredited Whigs. Russell, Monmouth, and others were averse to such an extreme course; and Shaftesbury, no longer able to rely on the adherence of London, fled to Holland, where he died in 1683.

Attack on Shaftesbury, 1681.

But his fiery spirit, which had already ruined the movement, lived on in a more desperate body of men. An attempt was made by some extreme members of the rank and file of the Whigs to settle the whole question by a plot to assassinate Charles and his brother. The plan—happily an abortive one—

The Rye House Plot, June, 1683.

was to waylay the victims at the Rye House on their way from Newmarket. This naturally caused all who had been connected with the recent agitation to be suspected. Russell and Algernon Sydney were tried and executed, though there was no evidence to connect them with the murderous plan. But the laws of treason were severely administered, and the known opinions of these men, evidenced in Sydney's case by some unpublished writings declaring the right to resist a bad king, were sufficient to bar all hope of acquittal. Monmouth was banished, and the great agitation which had threatened to sweep away the Stewart theory of Divine Right was at an end.

In the moment of triumph, when four years had elapsed without a parliament, with the Opposition discredited and crushed, the skilful victor died. The Roman Catholics, for whom he had risked so much and achieved so little, had the satisfaction of receiving Charles into their communion on his deathbed. As he was calm and collected amid the crises and agitations of his political life, so his perfect manners, quiet humour, and unflinching courage in the midst of great pain, lasted to the end. After apologizing to those who stood around for the "unconscionable time" which he took in dying, Charles expired on February 6, 1685. *Death of the king, 1685.*

CHAPTER VIII.

JAMES II.: 1685–1689.

James came to the throne as the hero of a victory which others had won. The Whigs were crushed. The attack on Hereditary Right was now but an episode in a discredited movement, the cry of a fallen party. The reaction in favour of monarchy was as complete at the end of Charles' reign as it had been in 1660. Indeed it was, in a sense, stronger, for it was the result of a double *The situation at home;*

lesson: the threats of the "Exclusionists" had reminded men of the anarchy of the Rebellion. Yet this reaction was not at bottom so much in favour of the crown as for the cause of peace.

Louis XIV. was now paramount in Europe; all other nations saw a menace to their safety in his illimitable claims and his unscrupulous raids. Pope and Emperor alike longed to check him. And one stern young Prince had long ago set his face like a flint towards the French frontiers, and meant to stem the tide of conquest. William of Orange had a double interest in England. To her he looked, as champion of Dutch independence, for that assistance against France, without which his determination to die on the last dyke was likely to be realized. To her he looked, as the Princess Mary's husband, for a kingdom whose resources he might use when his wife should in due course become Queen.

abroad.

The new king was 52 years old. He was a hard worker, a man of business, an experienced soldier, sailor, and administrator. He was without the lazy hesitancy of his grandfather, and lacked the noble resignation of his father, while he possessed to the full the obstinate belief in the Stewart mission, which had clogged the one and ruined the other. Moreover, he had developed the Stewart want of tact quite as much as his brother had avoided it. In fact he had a great deal of experience with none of its fruits. No character could make a man more unfit to be a king. When he persisted in a wrong course it was with a blind infatuation. What, then, was he likely to do with the grand opportunity to which he succeeded?

James' character and aims.

He reigned barely four years. In that short time he managed to alienate the Church of England, which had preached Divine Right and Non-Resistance for nearly a century; to restore the Whig party to a supremacy which lasted for upwards of 80 years; and finally to uproot his own dynasty from its firm hold in the hearts of the English people. Under James

Character of the reign.

the fear of a Popish king vanquished the fear of a civil war.

The reason is to be sought, like the clue to most of the seventeenth century problems, in Religion; James was a bigoted Roman Catholic, and while he persecuted to the death Presbyterians in Scotland, he determined to remove all restrictions on the political and religious position of the Roman Catholics in England. The laws which had been passed against Nonconformists of all sorts fall into two clear divisions. First, the *penal laws*, which forbade and punished the exercise of their religion; secondly, the *Tests*, which refused them all political and military office, unless they denied by word and deed their dearest beliefs. The former involved religious persecution, the latter political death. The Penal Laws might perhaps, in a short time, have been mitigated; for they were cruel and bloody, and many enlightened men disliked them. Meanwhile there would have been little difficulty in using the "Prerogative of Dispensing" to pardon those who were threatened with the more terrible punishments. Gradually men would have learned that punishment for religious opinion is no part of man's duty to man or to God. But the Tests, on the other hand, were considered by the majority, in the case of the Roman Catholics, as necessary for the national safety; and, in the case of Protestant Dissenters, as a useful means of keeping enemies out of power. James's attempts to break down the barriers which divided his co-religionists from the best and highest places in the land are the main feature of his reign. Like Charles, he relied on Louis' gold and on an army; but, unlike Charles, he had no idea what things were possible and what were not. James pursued his schemes till an exasperated nation called and welcomed his nephew and son-in-law to deliver it. Then he fled. No doubt Toleration was a good object, but Englishmen had reason to distrust Roman Catholics, who aimed at supremacy, and had perpetually endeavoured since the Reformation to overthrow the government by conspiracy or by open force.

When James found the nation resolute against his plan he endeavoured to carry it out against their will and their laws. Thus the Revolution which ensued turned on the old question—Is the king a *personal* ruler and above the law of the land? This question was at last to be answered in the negative.

The first and only Parliament of the reign was strongly loyal, but James was to find it still more strongly allied with the existing form of church government. The king promised to maintain the church and keep the laws, but had already received a large present from Louis, and informed that king's envoy that he relied on his master's help. Parliament voted a large increase of the royal revenue, though James had been taking ungranted customs. There was but one member who raised his voice in opposition to the crown, and he gained no supporters.

First meeting of Parliament. May, 1685.

Already a rebellion had occurred in Scotland. Archibald Earl of Argyle, son of the great Covenanter who had been beheaded in 1660, had landed in the Western Highlands early in 1685 to rouse his countrymen in defence of their religion; but the scheme was badly organized, and the rising was easily suppressed. A far more dangerous foe was now in arms in the South. The Duke of Monmouth, the natural son of the late king, had been living in Holland, where he was surrounded by many refugees of the old Exclusion and Whig party. Relying on his undoubted popularity in England he now landed at Lyme Regis (June, 1685), and declared for a free Parliament and relief of Dissenters. He received no support from the Prince of Orange, who was not likely to compromise his future by such a scheme. At Taunton the invader was proclaimed as King, but after a brief moment of success his followers were cut to pieces on Sedgmoor (July 6). He was captured and executed, after a piteous appeal to his uncle's mercy. His adherents, and all who had been concerned in the rising, were cruelly punished by the soldiers of Colonel Kirke and the judicial murders of Chief-justice Jeffreys,

The rising of Monmouth. June, 1685.

A STORMY PROSPECT.

who conducted the memorable "Bloody Assize" in the south-western counties with reckless blood-thirstiness.

This complete victory was a new advantage for the crown. Monmouth had corroborated the suspicions of those who had feared the "brisk boys" of Shaftesbury, and a third object lesson had thus confirmed the loyalty of all moderate men. But James drew the wrong lesson from his easy victory.

He was able indeed to increase his army as a measure of security. But when in November, 1685, the second session of Parliament opened, it was found that Halifax, whose tongue had saved the king in the Exclusion debate, had already been dismissed from office. *Second Session of Parliament.* James had appointed Roman Catholics to military posts from which they were excluded by the Test Act, and now announced to Parliament his intention to keep them there. Halifax had refused to vote for the repeal of the Act, and James meant to get that repeal from a Parliament of zealous churchmen. This proved to be quite impossible, and thus the most loyal Parliament a Stewart ever had was prorogued, as it proved, never to meet again.

Yet there was no sign that the king would moderate his course. His chief advisers were Roman Catholics— Father Petre, a Jesuit, Tyrconnel, a reckless Irish noble, and others. There were not wanting men who, while agreeing with James, hoped he would not rush headlong to his ruin by attacking the church. *Formation of parties.* Many moderate Roman Catholics were anxious to see him hold back, and Lawrence Hyde, Earl of Rochester, his own brother-in-law, a strong Tory and churchman, led a milder court party. But already there was forming an opposition, among men who were not inclined to take the royal assurance that promises should be kept as a sufficient national security. Halifax, Devonshire, and Compton, Bishop of London led this party. Thus we may say there were three divisions—the Jesuit cabal, the moderate Court party, and the opposition. The meaning of Roman Catholic toleration and the reliance to be placed upon royal promises were being illustrated just now in France, where Louis in 1685 rescinded the Edict of Nantes, which had given security to French Protestants for nearly a hundred years. This was unfortunate for James, since it quickened the sympathies and the fears of Englishmen.

The infatuated king meanwhile determined to prevent Parliament from meeting till he had a better opinion of their intentions; and to enlighten them he determined to get his power to dispense with the Test Act recognized in a court of law. After carefully packing the bench of judges with men whose servility was beyond suspicion, the king was gratified by a favourable verdict. It was a bogus case. The servant of a Roman Catholic officer, Sir Edward Hales, was induced to sue him for damages, which any informer could obtain by proving that the Act had been broken. The king had, by a dispensation, given Hales leave to break the law. Thus the question to be decided was, whether such a dispensation was a valid defence in law against the claim for the informer's reward. It was decided by the judges, in words which made the king a present of the English constitution, that the dispensation was quite valid. This dispensing power was certainly legal, but Charles II. had been warned by Parliament that it was not looked upon with any favour, and James was using it to accomplish an object which he had not dared to ask from Parliament rather than to mitigate the severities of the ordinary laws. It had been frequently used to save men from the rigours of the penal laws; but now it was to be openly used to evade the Tests.

Godden v. Hales. June, 1686.

A few days later another blow was struck at the Constitution as defined by Parliament. A court of Ecclesiastical Commission, much resembling that which had been abolished in 1641, was set on foot. James wished to punish Bishop Compton for refusing to suspend the Dean of Norwich, who had, contrary to royal orders, preached against the Roman Catholic faith. The powers granted to this royal commission

Revival of High Commission Court.

were the old spiritual powers wrested from the Pope by Henry VIII. James was not afraid to put back our history for 150 years by using them to further the Papal cause against the laws of England. Compton was suspended from his sacred functions. Such open measures were not tamely acquiesced in, and least of all by the suspended bishop, who was not of a submissive turn of mind. Riots occurred in London, and the short-sighted king established a large camp of soldiers under carefully chosen Popish officers on Hounslow Heath to keep his capital in awe.

A futile attempt to bend the Scots Parliament to that submission which he could no longer, at the moment, expect from England failed to show the king the folly of his course; and the beginning of 1687 found him still determined to go on. *A change of policy. 1687.* The Hydes, Clarendon (eldest son of the famous chancellor) and Rochester, were dismissed from office, as they were not to be induced to change their religion. Clarendon, who had been Lord Lieutenant of Ireland, was succeeded by the rampant Romanist Tyrconnel. This pointed clearly to the complete triumph of the Jesuit party at court. But it was also the beginning of a great change of policy: the king had tried to get his way with Parliament and with the moderate party, represented by Tories and high churchmen; he now determined to dissolve Parliament, and rely on the Dissenters rather than on the Church party. It was hoped that, if he offered them toleration, they would be prepared to assist him against the church by letting him raise Roman Catholics, as well as themselves, to civil and military office. For the Dissenters could not be expected to love the church, whose persecuting sons had shaped the "Clarendon Code" of 1664. James also calculated that the church, pledged to the doctrine that it was sinful to resist the king, might be insulted with impunity; though it might sulk it would, he thought, never rebel.

In accordance with this new plan the famous Declaration of Indulgence was issued in April, 1687. The penal laws and Tests were alike suspended. The Parliament would not repeal them, so the king did so himself. Roman Catholics and Protestant Dissenters were relieved of their civil disabilities, and allowed the free exercise of their religion. Charles II., in 1672, had only dared to suspend the penal laws, and had been compelled to give up the attempt. James had gone further, and in defiance of the clearest expression of the national opinion had set himself against the most rooted prejudices of his people. The question seemed no longer to be whether there should be Toleration, but whether there should be laws at all.

<small>The "Declaration".</small>

All now depended on the attitude of the Protestant Dissenters. If they were willing to accept a Toleration, which the king's whole life proved to be insincere, because it suited him, then the cause of church and law might fall together. Some of the leading Dissenters, such as William Penn, the Quaker, were closely allied with the king. But many notable Presbyterians, especially Baxter, were not likely to believe in the royal promises or desert the cause of national liberty for a momentary relief. Halifax, who had the keenest intellect of the day, issued a pamphlet[1] showing that the Dissenters, who were to be "hugged" now that they might be "squeezed" later on, were not the king's choice but his refuge; he implored them not to accept a brief against Magna Carta and destroy all laws in order to get relieved of one. They had a better chance, he urged, by waiting till the "next probable Revolution". The Dissenters were true to the cause of liberty, and in large numbers refused to show their preference of "infallibility" to "liberty".

<small>The Dissenters.</small>

By way of attacking the English Church in its most vital source the king next proposed to place his religion on an equality with Anglicanism in the Universities. The laws forbade men to hold college preferment without taking the oath of supremacy and other tests. Already Roman Catholic heads had

<small>The Church attacked.</small>

[1] Letter to a Dissenter, 1687.

been appointed to two Oxford colleges, University and Christ Church, and the vice-chancellor at Cambridge suspended for refusing to grant a degree to a monk. In the summer of 1687 James insisted that the Fellows of Magdalen College, Oxford, should elect as their president his nominee. When they resisted he secured their expulsion, and turned the college into a " Popish seminary". Preparations were now made for a Parliament, in which the king, by " packing ", hoped to secure a majority for his schemes. But the attempt to obtain promises and subservient candidates was a failure. And the astute Halifax came forward to show that the king's promise to substitute some other guarantee for the present laws against Roman Catholics was not an " equivalent ", since, if he did not respect laws which were already made, he would not respect laws which were yet to be made. The royal anger was preferable, urged this writer, to the national ruin.

In the year 1688 came the two events which strained the loyalty of the nation beyond its limits. The king's order in council (May, 1688) that the "Declaration" should be publicly read in church nerved the bishops to a memorable resistance. *The Crisis. 1688.* The birth of an heir to the throne in June led all classes of Englishmen to look over-sea to Holland for help, since a peaceful change upon James' death was no longer possible, after the appearance of a Popish heir.

Sancroft, Archbishop of Canterbury, and six bishops, after a meeting at Lambeth, signed a petition to James against his order in council. Relying upon their determination to resist, clergymen in *Trial of the seven bishops.* all parts of the country had refused to read the Declaration in compliance with that order. James was furious at this manifestation of hostility where he had expected obedience, and determined to prosecute the seven bishops for addressing " a false, malicious, and seditious libel " to their king. After a trial, watched with breathless interest by the entire nation, they were acquitted. It was argued by Somers, a young Whig lawyer, that the subject had a right to petition the crown, and that the document in question was neither false, nor malicious, nor seditious, nor a libel. The manifestations of delight with which the verdict was greeted in London and the country would have been sufficient warning to most men. Even the soldiers at Hounslow threw up their hats.

Almost at the same moment a letter was sent to William of Orange, inviting him to come and deliver the land from the galling bonds of a Popish Prince. A few leading men, Devonshire, Compton, Russell, and others, signed this letter and promised a favourable reception. The task was not an easy one for William. The little Prince was not believed to be the son of James and his Queen; but, apart from the revolutionary movement which the deposition of a tyrant and the dispossession of his heir involved, there were other difficulties. William could not risk a battle between English soldiers and Dutch troops, which would have stirred the patriotism of all people against a foreign invasion. He could not leave his loved Dutch frontiers at the mercy of the dragoons of Louis XIV. He was not sure that Tories in England would combine with Whigs to dispossess a monarch whom they considered as the Lord's Anointed. He could not reckon on supplies from the Dutch burghers, many of whom had no great love for his name and his house. Yet for William the chance had come. James could go no further and the iron was hot. He determined to strike. Louis, who wished to keep James above water lest England should be united and strong enough to interfere abroad, was nevertheless short-sighted enough to send, just at the wrong moment, all his forces to attack the districts of the Upper and Middle Rhine.

William invited to interfere. June 30, 1688.

William's difficulties.

Thus relieved, the Whig Deliverer landed at Torbay, November 5, 1688. James had made some efforts at conciliation, but to little purpose. The bishops refused to exhort the nation not to resist their king. In a short while the invader was joined by the foremost Whigs; and a large part of the army,

The landing of William.

THE REVOLUTION.

under the influence of Churchill, the future Duke of Marlborough, who had been sent to Salisbury to oppose William, deserted the Royal cause. As the invader drew nearer London James, after sending his wife and child to France, endeavoured to follow them; but he was captured and brought back to the capital. William had not claimed the kingdom, but had merely declared in favour of a free Parliament and Toleration, with a maintenance of the Tests and other bulwarks against Popery. Nothing was settled, though bloodshed had been avoided. The next step was critical. It was an anxious moment for all.

James was told that he could not stay in London, and was allowed to select a place of refuge. He chose Rochester, and promptly fled thence to France. This altered the character of the Revolution. *The Revolution, 1688.* Tories, who held that no violence to a king was possible, would have been relieved from many scruples if they could honestly have considered that James had vacated his post. But it was obvious that he had been obliged to go, and it was no secret that he was in fear of personal violence. Thus the Revolution, which had begun in an alliance of Whigs and Tories, became a Whig victory, from which it at first appeared that all true Tories must stand aloof. The Whigs held that a bad king had no rights, and said as much.

William took the government into his hands at the invitation of the peers, who advised that a Convention Parliament should be summoned. The surviving members of some of Charles the Second's *The Convention. 1689.* Parliaments were also called, and gave the same advice. On February 1, 1689, this memorable assembly met at Westminster. It contained in the lower House a majority for the Whigs, who meant to change the succession. But in the Lords there was a Tory majority, still hampered by the difficulty of reconciling their theory of Non-Resistance and Passive Obedience with a Revolution. Some were for appointing William Regent for James, while others argued that James was dead to the constitution and his daughter Mary was already Queen by hereditary right. Finally, after much debate and many searchings of heart, it was declared that James having broken "the original contract between king and people and withdrawn himself out of the kingdom, has abdicated the government, and the throne is thereby vacant". The scruples of the Tories had been removed by William's announcement that he would go home unless they made him King, and that he would not stay here as his wife's "gentleman usher". William and Mary were promptly declared King and Queen of England.

The Revolution was a compromise. The Whigs secured the insertion into the Constitution of their theory that government is a contract and not an heirloom in any family. The Tories were allowed to make-believe that James had left them no other course by his flight. After a brief discussion about the conditions on which the new rulers should be received, it was decided to draw up a "Declaration of Right", which, when the Convention had decided to continue its own existence as a legal Parliament, was passed into law as the "Bill of Rights". This famous document asserted most clearly that the law was sovereign in England by enumerating the acts by which James had exasperated the nation, and declaring them, one by one, to be illegal. This was the solution of the problem which had pressed for an answer for so long. Henceforth there could be in no part of the constitution a claim to set aside a law when duly passed by King, Lords, and Commons. The right to act in virtue of a "discretionary" power, which was summed up in the words *Salus populi suprema lex*, was to be heard of no more. The motto which the Stewarts had tried to affix to the English constitution must, after the Revolution, be read *Lex suprema populi salus*.

<small>Character of the constitutional change.</small>

CHAPTER IX.

WILLIAM III.: 1689–1702.

William, Prince of Orange, and Stadtholder of the United Provinces, was now King of England, not as Mary's husband, but together with her as the chosen successor of James. He was just forty years old, and had profited by his experience in a way that was to make him able to rule England and play the foremost part in European politics. It has been said that William was never young. He had been born and bred amid intrigues, revolutions, plots; and had grown to manhood with the roar of French guns in his ears. He was cold and hard in manner, had wretched health, and was personally unattractive. *The new king.*

His ambition had been to make himself and his beloved Holland a power in Europe, and his chance had been so opportunely seized that he now hoped to add the name and resources of England to that League of Augsburg which the restless Louis XIV. had roused against himself in 1686. The Pope, the numerous German princes, the Emperor, and the King of Spain had long been anxious to check the daring monarch who swooped down now on the Pyrenees, now on Italy, now on the Rhine or the Sambre. If William, backed by the English nation and the English navy, could lead the way, there would be some chance of making headway even against so great a power as that wielded by Louis. *His aims.*

The austere and forbidding nature of the new king was thus redeemed by one splendid passion, love for Holland and all that Holland meant upon the map of Europe. But he was also a man of the most dauntless courage, displayed alike on the field and in the council. No military reverse could diminish it, no political difficulties limit it. And he needed it all. For in England he found not enthusiasm or reverence for *William and his prospects in England.*

the deliverer, but much treachery and more distrust. Only where he could make them see that he was working for their own immediate interests, or when Louis put a trump card into his hand by attack or insult, did the English nation rally round William. They were jealous of his Dutch favourites; they knew he loved the gardens of Loo better than all the attractions of Kensington, and that he neither loved nor admired Englishmen, except indeed when he watched their corpses being piled beneath the walls of a French fortress.

But more than this. England was, so far as concerns her government, in a stage of transition. The "king above the law" was no more. But the "law above the king" was not a condition of things which could be easily substituted for the old Stewart theory in a few weeks. Parliament was strong, and divided into two hostile camps of Whig and Tory. The Tories disliked William and felt ashamed of themselves for their revolutionary conduct. The Whigs hated the Tories and thought William should follow their example. The king had no mind to become a tool of the Whigs, and hoped to keep both in order by playing one party against the other. But he could only do so by retaining some of his kingly power, and thus he gave some sections of both parties a chance to combine against him. Nowadays the sovereign remains in the background, while the ministries, composed on strict party lines, replace each other when the nation is dissatisfied with the party in power. But this "Cabinet government" was not, in William's day, more than an occasional expedient, and the nation had not yet learnt its power to make its wishes felt.

Changes in the English constitution.

Thus Parliament was more powerful than was just then desirable. It was free from the king, without being subject to the nation. The king could only manage it by choosing ministers whom it would support, thus beginning that system which is now always in operation—government by a cabinet with a majority in Parliament to pass its measures. William was, throughout his reign, obliged to rush backwards and forwards from the Dutch frontiers to London, to work a machine without which he could do nothing, yet which frequently thwarted his best endeavours.

His greatest difficulty, however, arose from his own insecure position: few believed that, with a divided nation, and a greedy, watchful enemy, who announced his intention by word and deed to restore the fallen Stewart, William could long remain King of England. The Jacobites, as the adherents of James and his descendants were called, were powerful and alert. Every victory of France on the Continent sent a thrill of treason through the English politicians who watched the great game. It is disappointing to find statesmen of all shades of opinion involved in this treachery; with very few exceptions they corresponded secretly with James at St. Germains, where he now kept up regal state at the expense of the King of France. William knew and understood this, and it is not the least part of his title to fame that he not only refused to take vengeance, but actually contrived to work with men of whose letters to the exile he had copies in his hands. *Insecurity breeds treason.*

We may divide the reign into five periods. The first two years (1689–1691) were occupied with the settlement of Scotland and Ireland, for James and Louis made a great attempt to keep William out of their path by giving him work in Ireland. This expedient would, if successful, have tied the king's hands very effectually. But all fears of a Jacobite Ireland were allayed by the battle of the Boyne. From 1692 to 1695 William struggled unsuccessfully with his great foe on the Continent, while he contrived to keep his government efficient at home by intrusting more and more power to the Whigs. The death of Queen Mary marks the close of this second period. The third consists of two years (1695–1697) in which the power of France was successfully tired out, while the continued domination of the Whigs secured a strong war policy. With the Peace of Ryswick (1697) the nation, led by Tories, ceased to support William; and in the fourth period (1697–1701) his parliaments became more and more unmanageable, while on the Continent the tardy *Periods of the reign.*

death of the Spanish king raised the greatest political problem of the age. Just as the French king was about to seize all those gains which the English jealousy against William was pouring into his hands, the death of James II. occurred. The recognition of his son as King of England, which Louis promptly made, once more stung the English into a warlike temper. The fifth period (1701–1702) therefore shows us William and his adopted country again at one, but with the last and fiercest struggle still to come. At this moment William died.

The "Convention" was, at the commencement of the reign, made into a legal and competent Parliament, and **Settlement of the kingdom.** continued in session. William wished to secure a moderate settlement of religion and finance, so that all faithful men might serve the state and the state might be strong against France. But no such simple solution was possible. The Toleration Act (1689) was passed, but gave only relief from penal laws to those Protestant dissenters who were prepared to take the oaths of allegiance and supremacy. No tests or penal laws were done away with. It was toleration in partial practice without the principle. There was no chance of "comprehension",—the reconciliation of Protestant nonconformists to the Church of England—though William wished it and Convocation discussed it. The new oath of allegiance to William and Mary was made compulsory for all officers in church or state, and those who refused to take it, the "Non-jurors", as they are called, lost their posts. Sancroft, the hero of the resistance to James's Declaration, led a party of non-juring bishops, and was deprived of his archbishopric. The revenue was settled on William, but Parliament considered it necessary to assert the principles of the constitution by granting it only for one year at a time. The Whig section now began to show a violent party spirit. They tried to secure their own domination by punishing those who had abetted James's illegal acts, especially those who had surrendered the charters of corporations to the last two kings. This, together with their resistance to the Bill of Indemnity, which was to pardon the past, caused a dissolution. In March, 1690, a new Parliament, with a larger preponderance of Tories, gave the king a firmer position and enabled him, to some extent, to hold the balance of parties. His ministers were drawn from both sections, the chief being Godolphin, Shrewsbury, Nottingham, Halifax, and Danby.

Meanwhile in Ireland William's presence had become necessary. James, assisted by the French, had landed there in March, 1689; and at once the national feeling, so long repressed by the system which Cromwell established in the English and Protestant interest, sprang to life. James was welcome as a Roman Catholic, but the Irish thought more of securing their independence of those who had taken their land and proscribed their religion, than of restoring the king. The Protestants intrenched themselves in Londonderry and Enniskillen, while the Irish Parliament set to work to undo the settlement of 1660. *The struggle in Ireland.*

Londonderry was relieved in July, 1689, after 105 days of siege and suffering; but Marshal Schomberg, whom William sent over with a small army, failed to secure Dublin. Thus in June, 1690, William, who then landed in Ireland with large reinforcements, had to face the whole rebellion with James still at its head. With such a coward as James, however, the issue could not long be doubtful. The decisive battle took place near Drogheda, where James hoped to defend his position behind the Boyne. The river was crossed and the position was stormed on July 1, 1690. James fled to France in craven haste. The fall of Limerick a year later completed the defeat of the Irish. Again the country was given up to the Protestant and English settlers, who, at once, more than restored the system of 1660, and utterly excluded the Roman Catholics from political power and social consideration.

The French, who had for the moment a sufficient advantage at sea to make communication between England and Ireland impossible, had not managed to do so. But though William was allowed to cross, the error was partly retrieved by their occupation of the Channel, whence they drove Lord Torrington and his fleet after an engagement at Beachy Head, June 30, 1690. The English fleet, though chased to the Thames, was still powerful, and as the cause of James in Ireland was already lost, this reverse did little for the Jacobites. In truth there ought to have been such a French fleet in existence as would have kept William in England, enabled James to hold Ireland, and succoured the Jacobites in Scotland.

The struggle in the Channel.

For here, too, there was a party for the late king. The Covenanters, forced in 1660 to submit to the religious government they hated, had risen on James's fall, and in a Convention (March, 1689) abolished Episcopacy and proclaimed William and Mary. But the Highlanders had been raised in the Jacobite interest by Graham of Claverhouse, better known as Viscount Dundee, who roused the clans that hated the Covenanting tribe of the Campbells, the great supporters of Whiggery, to fight for King James. They won a battle at Killiecrankie Pass in July, 1689, but lost their leader, and with the fickleness that Celtic hosts have always shown, they at once dispersed. William endeavoured, when this formidable rising was over, to settle Scotland by establishing the Presbyterian form of church government. His efforts to stop the persecution of Episcopal clergy were in a great measure successful, and redound to his credit; though we cannot acquit him of all blame for the dastardly way in which the Macdonalds of Glencoe were murdered in the beginning of 1692. Their chief had failed to comply with an order that all clans were to submit to the government by January 1. His submission a few days later was refused, and William signed an order for the extermination of the clan, which was carried out by brutal treachery instead of by military execution.

The Scottish rising.

By the summer of 1691 William was able to commence his great struggle with France. The allies were already in arms, and some fighting had taken place on various parts of the French frontiers. The war is not interesting,

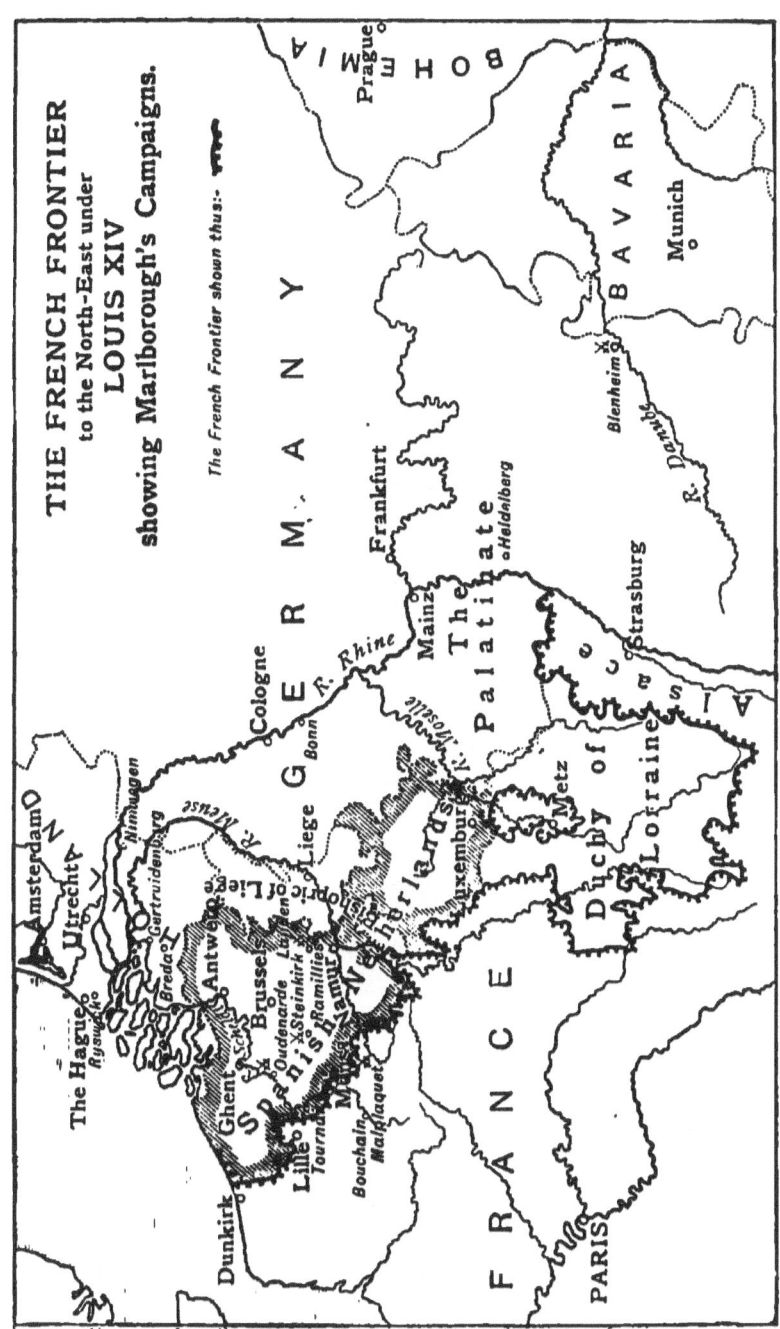

for it consisted, so far as William was concerned, in a stern struggle to keep his allies true to their promises and his parliaments to their interests, and in marching out to meet the French armies, which were personally conducted by Louis so long as only sieges and no battles took place. For when he could not hold a brilliant court round some starving garrison, the French king left his generals to fight the King of England. As William was a very unlucky commander, the advantages he secured by diplomacy among his allies and at Westminster were not infrequently lost when he faced a French army, led by such a general as Luxembourg. But though often out-manœuvred and sometimes routed, William's true greatness always appeared more splendidly in defeat than in victory. Each summer a campaign took place, and it was merely a question which could continue to put men and money into the business longest. If the alliance broke up, or the Parliament refused supplies, William must lose; if France sickened with exhaustion he might win.

Character of the war on the Continent.

In 1691 William arrived on the frontiers only to find that the fortress of Mons had passed into the hands of the French king (April, 1691). He left a parliament recently nerved to vote supplies by the burning of Teignmouth, which had followed the naval defeat of Beachy Head. But a network of Jacobite intrigue was spreading, and while men like Russell, the seaman, and Marlborough, the soldier, were content with sending their expressions of duty and service to James, the more active members of the party prepared plans for a rising, while on the French shores armies were being collected for an attack upon England.

Campaign of 1691.

In May, 1692, the French fleet was beaten and destroyed off Cape La Hogue by Russell, who was not ashamed to write letters to James pleading the excuse that his professional reputation was at stake in the matter. The descent upon England was thus put out of the question. This was a sufficient revenge for the defeat at Beachy Head, and France gave

Campaign of 1692, 1693.

us little more trouble by sea. Meanwhile the French king and his court were watching the siege of Namur, which surrendered in June, 1692. William, who arrived too late to save it, was then badly beaten by Luxembourg at Steenkerke (August, 1692). A second serious defeat at Landen in the following July brought the military prospects of the Allies very low.

But in England matters were improving. The factious spirit in Parliament was shown when the Whigs, jealous of the Tories, proposed the Triennial Bill, which would put an end to William's plan of getting a ministry to manage the Parliament for as long a time as he could. *Whigs gain ground, 1693-1694.* A general election every three years would give the party out of power a better chance; the bill was passed, but was rejected by William, who thus exercised his legal power of refusing to assent to a bill. But the Whigs were too strong to be neglected, and, as a compromise, their champion Somers was made Lord Keeper of the Seal, while the Tory Nottingham had to resign. Sunderland, who was able to give good advice, though unable to keep true to any principles, suggested to William to make a united Whig ministry, and so keep his Parliament in good humour. The Tories, who had been in the ascendant for the last few years, were losing ground. They had no hearty belief in the war, and their lack of energy in its conduct was a source of failure. The Whigs were also fortunate in securing at this time the strongest support they ever had, the commercial interest of England; not only those merchants whose ships had been lost when in 1693 the Smyrna fleet was captured and its convoy dispersed by the French; but all those who were concerned in the new financial expedients. For it was an age of financial expedients; a young and clever Whig named Montague had succeeded in raising loans for the war expenses by setting up the Bank of England. This meant that a body of men who negotiated the loans received from government privileges, by which they were enabled to secure a practical monopoly of the lucrative business of money-lending. The Tories soon grew jealous of this power. For it played into the Whig hands by firmly attaching those men who lent the money to the government, from which alone they could hope for payment. They tried to secure similar advantages by what is known as the Land Bank. This was an absurd scheme for making money by the wholesale lending or mortgaging of land: but as many people wanted to borrow money and few to borrow land, the Bank of England won the day, and soon became a powerful and important Whig institution.

With Montague chancellor of the exchequer, and his financial success on every tongue, the campaign of 1694 was opened; nothing beyond an unsuccessful attack upon the French harbour of Brest need be mentioned. The Whigs were able to secure the Triennial Act, for William did not care to veto it a second time; it looked as if the war would be waged with vigour, and the party strife at home be ended by the domination of the Whigs and the war party.

The Whig successes.

At this moment a great blow fell upon William. His wife, to whom he was sincerely attached, died suddenly of small-pox in December, 1694. This blow, from which it seemed at first as if the king himself would scarcely rally, for a time seriously menaced his political position. Mary's presence upon the throne of her ancestors had in fact been a rallying point for Tories and High Churchmen. It had been the means of securing a larger number of adherents for government, both in and out of Parliament, than could have been hoped for had William been without the much-needed aid of her popularity, sweet temper, and good sense. But the fall of Danby, one of the last surviving Tory ministers, who was at this time accused of receiving bribes from the East India Company, brought the Whigs further to the front, and their combination was strong enough to stand the strain.

Death of Mary.

The third period of the reign was the most successful for William. Godolphin was now the only Tory minister. Mary's sister, the Princess Anne, who had been estranged from the court by the jealous intrigues of her friend the

Countess of Marlborough, was now reconciled to William; though Marlborough was in disgrace owing to his dealings with St. Germains. Great financial efforts were made, and in August, 1695, William had the satisfaction of retaking Namur. *Vigorous policy at home and abroad.* With this decided success to back him the king returned and dissolved Parliament, with a view to gaining a further Whig success in the elections. He made a real effort to secure personal popularity by making a "progress" through the country, visiting large towns, and staying in the country houses of important men. The Whigs were largely victorious at the polls, and a liberal war grant followed. But there was also plenty of work to be done at home. A bill to make trials for high treason more humane, by allowing the prisoner to have the same legal advantages as in other trials, was passed. The Whig financiers, Somers and Montague, assisted by Locke and Sir Isaac Newton, carried through a much-needed scheme for amending the coinage. A sound currency is the condition of a sound commerce, and the Whigs, who were supported by the "monied interest", replaced the old thin and clipped silver by new and thicker coins of full weight.

The French were not inactive, in spite of the fall of Namur and the death of their best general, Luxembourg. Louis was willing to assist any rising in England, and James's illegitimate son, the Duke of Berwick, crossed the Channel in disguise. *Jacobite troubles.* But he found that, like the French, the English Jacobites wished to see the others make the first move. There was no general rising, and Louis was too business-like a plotter not to require something solid for his money. Early in 1696, however, a plot was formed among some desperate men to attack and murder William when he went hunting at Richmond. Fortunately a large party had to be enrolled in order to overcome his guards, and·there was a fair sprinkling of traitors among these would-be assassins. The plot was betrayed, and the result was all in William's favour. An association was formed, and swore to defend the king and maintain the succession of the Princess Anne. Thus the Whigs won all along the line, and in 1697 William had a completely Whig ministry, a fairly loyal nation, and a Parliament ready to work with the government.

It was now clear that France was terribly exhausted by the gigantic efforts she had made to keep up the war along her entire frontier. The King of England might therefore take advantage of this either to secure a peace or to strike a blow. The former would disarm his foes at home, who relied upon French assistance, and William opened negotiations. It was finally arranged that the French king should recognize William as King of England and Anne as his successor. He was to give up all that he had taken or conquered since the peace of 1678, with the important exception of Strasbourg, which he insisted on retaining. (Sept. 10, 1697.).

Peace of Ryswick.

The retention of this fortress was, however, a very trifle compared to the enormous accession of territory that Louis hoped to acquire on the death of Charles II. of Spain. It was now plain that the feeble life of that monarch was drawing to a close, and Europe was awed into a calm at the thought of the vastness of the issues at stake. It was during this calm—the fourth period of the reign—that Louis and William endeavoured to avert the threatening storm, by a scheme for the Partition of the hereditary dominions of the Spanish crown. There were numerous claimants, but the great question lay between the Imperial or Austrian house and that of the Bourbons. The three royal houses of Spain, France, and Austria were united by various complicated intermarriages. But so far as blood was concerned the Dauphin had a clear right to the whole Spanish dominion, consisting of Spain, the Indies, Sicily, Naples, Milan and the Netherlands. The danger of so great an accession of power to France had long been foreseen, and by the Treaty of the Pyrenees (1659) Louis' wife had renounced all rights for herself and her descendants. The Dauphin's claim was there-

Spanish Succession problem.

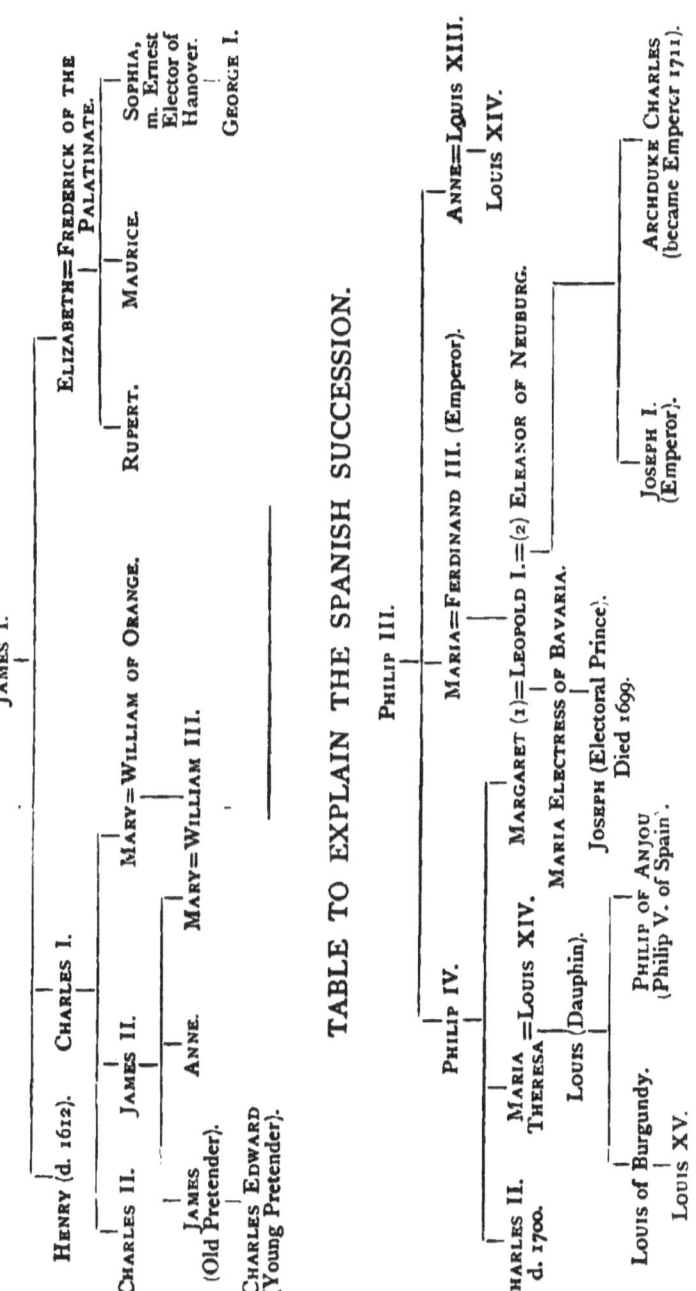

fore barred by international agreement. The Emperor Leopold I. had a claim through his mother, which, though not so good by pedigree, was hampered by no renunciation. A third claim passed to his daughter, the Electress of Bavaria, through her mother, the younger sister of Charles of Spain, but this was also barred by a treaty. The houses of Austria and France were each bound to resent so great a windfall coming to the other. The young Electoral Prince of Bavaria represented a third party, whose accession to the crown of Spain would at least keep out the direct heirs of both the rival powers. And it was upon him that the great inheritance was settled by the famous First Partition Treaty, arranged between William and Louis. English interests were concerned, inasmuch as the union or close alliance of Spain and France would be practically a veto upon English trade and commerce in the New World and the Mediterranean. Louis was anxious to keep Austria from the inheritance, and to secure a further slice of European territory without fighting for it. This arrangement, therefore, gave the Indies, Spain, and the Netherlands to the Bavarian prince. French ambition was allayed by the offer of Naples and Sicily, together with a small part of the north of Spain (Guipuscoa). The Archduke Charles, Leopold's younger son, received the Duchy of Milan. This seemed a fair way out of the terrible dilemma, but scarcely was it settled when the Bavarian prince died of small-pox, and the whole negotiation was rendered useless.

First Partition, 1698.

William had in his hands the whole management of these puzzling continental politics, but his next efforts to settle the matter out of court were cramped by the condition of affairs at home. No sooner was the Peace of Ryswick signed than the English nation ceased to support him. The tension of the continental struggle once over, a reaction began. The national fear and jealousy of a standing army broke out fiercely. There were three reasons why such a force was no longer dangerous as of old. William was not a James II.,

Reaction in England.

and had no quarrel with English laws. The rapacity of Louis made it absolutely necessary to treat with him sword in hand. The Mutiny Act (1689), by which Parliament granted special disciplinary powers over the army, was annually passed, and could be refused if the Houses had cause to distrust those who maintained the army. Without such powers no army could be kept in order.

But a Tory reaction was in progress, and the magnificent forces of William were reduced to 7000 men. The favourite Dutch guards were sent home, though the king made a pathetic appeal to be allowed to retain them. The expenses of the late war gave the Tories a handle, and they insisted on resuming large grants of crown lands which William had foolishly given in some profusion to Dutch favourites. Men thought more of the taxation which would follow a fresh outburst of war than of making such war impossible by a bold policy.

The death of Joseph of Bavaria made necessary a Second Partition Treaty, in which Louis found much advantage. The Archduke Charles was made heir to Spain and the Netherlands, which were both far enough from Austria to make this increase of Hapsburg power unimportant. Louis still received for his son Naples and Sicily, as well as Milan, which he hoped to exchange for Lorraine, a province long since practically his own by right of theft and occupation. *Second Partition, 1700.*

Hardly was this arranged when the unhappy prince, whose dominions were thus meted out, died in the Escurial, November, 1700. He had been persuaded at the last, by those who succeeded in gaining influence over his weak and tortured mind, to make a will, by which all his dominions were to pass to Louis' grandson, Philip, Duke of Anjou. Thus for a second time the labours and cares of months were thrown away, and Louis, lightly breaking his treaty and his promise, accepted the will. The Pyrenees, as he proudly boasted, existed no longer, and all Western Europe had become the heritage of the Bourbons. *Failure of William's policy.*

To William this was a severe blow. But the English

people refused to share his alarm. The Partition, with its addition to French power in the Mediterranean, was unpopular among the merchants, and they had little fear of a future policy so united on the part of France and Spain as to menace Europe in general or English ships in particular.

This was the darkest moment in William's reign. He had been tricked abroad, humiliated at home, and there appeared no way out of the difficulty. Moreover a succession difficulty seemed about to threaten in England itself. Anne's only son, the Duke of Gloucester, died in 1700; and as William's health was daily failing a new scheme of succession was absolutely necessary if Jacobite hopes were to be disappointed. Long ago it had been suggested that the crown should pass, after the death of Anne, to the family of Sophia, Electress of Hanover, who was a granddaughter of James I.[1] The Act of Settlement (1701) made this into law, and thus completed the work of the Revolution. The crown was to be strictly hereditary in the Hanoverian family, provided they were Protestants. At the same time the independence of the judges was secured; they were now to be removed only after an address from both Houses of Parliament, and several other important constitutional provisions added. But strong jealousy of the Dutch king and his favourites was still shown. The fears of William were, however, speedily justified. By the Peace of Ryswick Dutch soldiers were allowed to garrison certain fortresses on the frontiers of the Netherlands, since Spanish troops were neither efficient nor trustworthy. Louis in 1701 occupied these "Barrier Fortresses", and thus once more showed his contempt for the public law of Europe.

There was now no means of shirking the question of war. The commercial interest was alarmed and party strife ran high. The Tories were not inclined to yield their position when the war feeling began. They impeached four members of

[1] See p. 111.

William's government, and imprisoned some freeholders who presented the "Kentish Petition" in favour of war.

But for William, though he had been obliged to yield his dearest plans and see his efforts thwarted, fate had one triumph in store. In September, 1701, James II. died at St. Germains. The French king <small>Louis insults England.</small> had really only one more solemn engagement left to break. He seized this opportunity to break it, and ostentatiously recognized James's son, the Pretender, as King of England. This was enough to complete the overthrow of the Tories and to give William the enthusiasm he wished to rouse. Parliament was dissolved amid national clamours for war against the French. The Whigs, who gained the advantage at the polls, voted supplies and passed a bill to secure the Protestant succession. Once more the king had the English behind him. But for William there was to be no part in the mighty struggle which was now to break the power of his foe, and raise English arms and an English general to the highest pinnacle of military glory. A fall from his horse stretched him on a bed of sickness from which he never moved. At the very moment when one animated by a life-long passion for war against France would have most cared to live, William breathed his last at Kensington, on March 8, 1702.

CHAPTER X.

ANNE: 1702–1714.

Anne, the younger daughter of James II. by his first marriage, became queen on William's death by the express terms of the Revolution settlement. She was likely to be popular, for she was a Stewart, <small>The new queen.</small> and yet a sincere member of the Anglican Church. The Tories would see in her a representative of the family whose misdeeds they were so anxious to forgive. The Whigs would approve of a queen succeeding by laws framed against the enemies of England's liberties. She was a good woman without much will of her own. Thus it was easy to influence her. And it was necessary for those who wished to secure power to do so, for she retained a good deal of the importance in politics which had belonged to her predecessors. She sat in the council, and the ministers were her nominees, or the nominees of those who worked upon her feelings.

The constitution was, as we have seen, changing. A time was coming when the sovereign would be obliged to choose ministers trusted by the Commons and the country. The existence of parties had forced William to do so. This was becoming even more necessary in Anne's reign. Indeed, her greatest change of ministers in 1710 was the result of a national and party agitation which carried the queen along with it. This presents a great contrast to the early days of the period, when the Stewart kings had endeavoured to maintain ministers in opposition to the movement of the time. The extension of this system was destined in the end to solve the problem of English government. But meanwhile the fact remains that Anne was sufficiently her own mistress to be unwilling to make changes except under pressure. Thus her easily-led nature became a most important political matter. Her personal influence was perhaps heightened by the fact that her husband, Prince George of Denmark, was a man of no political weight. There was "nothing in him", according to Charles II., who professed to have "tried him drunk and tried him sober".

Her constitutional importance.

The reign is much less puzzling than that which preceded it. Three main problems, the European question, the position of Parliament in the state, and the permanence of the Revolution settlement, seem to come to a clear issue—an issue whose importance is none the less on account of its clearness.

Chief points of the reign.

The position of France on the Continent remained to be determined. It was a problem which had occupied the minds of statesmen since the end of the Thirty Years'

War in 1648. Louis XIV. had first tried to seize the Netherlands, and been checked by the Triple Alliance and the Peace of Aix-la-Chapelle. He had next tried to punish the Dutch, but had been forced to desist at the Peace of Nimuegen. His ambition, still unsatisfied by his gains, had then been confronted by a European coalition, which finally bound him by the Peace of Ryswick. Now was to come the war of the Spanish Succession, which was to break his proud spirit and rescue the Continent from the spectre of French domination which had haunted the imagination of Europe for fifty years. *(1) The European question.*

This foreign war carried the second problem with it. Whigs and Tories could not fight out their party struggle upon the question of Jacobitism; for the Pretender never wavered in his allegiance to Rome, and most Tory statesmen knew that a Roman Catholic king was out of the question, even if a son of James II. might otherwise have been desirable. But the Whig war and the Whigs who carried it on; the Dissenters who were still the friends of the Whigs; the "monied men" who supplied the Whig exchequer—these were always open to the Tory attack. The reign of Anne thus became a period of keen party struggle, complicated at every step by the military question on the Continent; a struggle carried on by any and every means, at the termination of which the great constitutional change had been brought far on its way. For, with a weak woman on the throne, it became only a battle of "ins" and "outs", of those who held power and those who wished to supplant them. Those who won must do so by having Parliament on their side. A pale reflection of such a struggle is witnessed now in our everyday political life. The difference is that, now, the whole nation, with its millions of voters and its hourly newspapers, watches, and finally decides the struggle at the polls; whereas in those days, though pamphlets issued rapidly from Whig pens and Tory pens, it took as many days as it now takes hours for the real truth concerning the parliamentary debates to penetrate to the *(2) The party struggle and its importance.*

ears even of the cultivated classes. The party that was out of power had to raise a cry sufficient to influence those few who had votes. It had also to secure the queen's ear by means of those who were about her. Yet, after the strides made in the direction of "Cabinet" government[1] between the Revolution and the accession of George I., the bringing of the will of the nation to bear on these matters was only a question of time. The control of government had passed for ever from the hands of the personal monarch. It was bound eventually to pass to the majority of the nation.

One more question, which had agitated England for a long time, was also to come up for solution. The Jacobites hoped that, though Anne might be permitted to reign, no German prince would ever succeed to the throne of the Stewart House. The Hanoverian succession was the law of the land, but whether it would be converted into a fact was in grave doubt during the last few years of Anne's life. Between a foreigner and a Roman Catholic the choice was not an easy one.

(3) The Succession problem.

With these three points before us—the European crisis, the party struggle, and the succession dilemma —the reign may be divided into three periods.

Three periods of the reign.

In the first (1702–1708) the European question was foremost. The national enthusiasm set the war going, and the genius of Marlborough made it successful. The queen was completely under the influence of the wife of her great commander; the Whigs secured a majority in Parliament, and the ministers were chosen from among them. Louis was beaten on all sides and sued for peace, which was at first refused. In the second period (1708–1710) the strife of parties at home is all-important. Wearied by the long war, the nation refused to support Marlborough, as they had refused to support William. The danger seemed over. The influence of the duchess was undermined, and Queen Anne ceased to take

---

[1] This means that the ministers are chosen entirely from the leaders of the party which has a majority in Parliament, and resign directly they lose that majority.

pleasure in the society of a "brawling woman in a wide house". A Tory reaction occurred. Churchmen raised their voices against toleration, and the foolish prosecution of one of them gave away the dignity of the government, who, their popularity being already gone, could not long hope to retain office. The struggle ended in a victory for the Tories, and thus incidentally for the principle of party government. A Tory ministry was soon appointed, and in the third period (1710-1714) the Revolution settlement trembled in the balance. Peace was made with France, a peace perhaps necessary, perhaps just, yet in terms far less·glorious than our victorious armies were considered to have earned. The Tory ministers plotted for a Tory triumph, perhaps for a Stewart Restoration. The death of Anne, however, found this ministry divided by a quarrel between its leaders, and the Whigs were able to obtain sufficient influence in the council to secure the succession of George I.

The war of the Spanish succession (1702-1713) was waged mainly in three separate quarters. First, on the eastern side of France, in the Netherlands, along the Rhine and the borders of Bavaria and Austria. Here Marlborough and his Dutch allies had to succour the Emperor, and to drive Louis from the Netherlands, which they had to regain foot by foot. Secondly, in Italy, where Eugene, a prince of the house of Savoy, faced the French armies sent into the Milanese Duchy, and endeavoured to prevent them from reaching Austria by the Tyrolese passes. Thirdly, in Spain itself, where the English, with their Spanish and Portuguese allies, endeavoured to drive Philip V. from his newly-acquired throne, and to place the Archduke Charles—the candidate of the Allies—in his place. This was the ostensible purpose for which the war was being waged, though it turned into a struggle to keep France from attacking the empire and the Netherlands, as well as from obtaining a commanding position in North Italy; the Spanish campaigns always remained of secondary importance.

Character of the war.

As William had died when war was popular there was no delay in taking up the struggle. Marlborough took com-
A promising opening. mand of the allies in the Netherlands, and war was formally declared in May, 1702. Anne was still as much as ever under the influence of this great man and his wife. The queen allowed her favourite to call her "Mrs. Morley", and, in the familiar intercourse between the friends, the duchess was "Mrs. Freeman". The ministry comprised both Whigs and Tories; Marlborough and Godolphin, to whom the former was related by marriage, being the leading spirits. Soon, however, it became clear that the Tories loved neither the war nor those who were conducting it, and they gradually were eliminated from the administration. Nottingham left office in 1704, and the Whigs Sunderland[1] and Somers soon appeared in the ministry. The elections in 1705 were in favour of the Whigs, and the gradual stiffening of the Whig element in the government reflected their gains in Parliament. Thus, for the first period of the reign, the war policy went smoothly enough at home. It will be well, therefore, to describe the main features of the military struggle.

The first necessity for Marlborough was to check the French advance towards the Dutch frontier, for Louis
Marlborough's objects. had already possession of most of the Spanish Netherlands. In 1702 the English general was occupied with the siege of several fortresses in order to construct the desired barrier. Liège was captured, and in 1703 he took Bonn, thus stretching his line considerably towards the Middle Rhine. Louis' main object, however, was not to expend strength on this frontier where English and Dutch stood firm. Between Eugene in Italy and Marlborough in Flanders lay a great tract of country, in which Louis' allies, the Bavarians, were for the moment dominant. It was, therefore, the object of the French to send forces through this great gap and attack the emperor in his hereditary dominion of Austria. He was the weakest member of the coalition;

---

[1] Son of the old minister of James II., but a strong Whig himself.

and, if Louis could seize Vienna as he had seized Strasbourg, he could dictate terms to one at least of the Allies. Prince Eugene won the battle of Cremona in 1702, and prevented the French, who held Milan, from pouring troops through the Tyrol to Austria. But the French attack was soon after made in the centre, where Marshal Tallard made a dash for the valley of the Upper Danube in 1704.

The King of France, however, had to deal with a man whose ordinary calm commonsense flashed into genius when a campaign or a battle was to be worked out or fought. Marlborough saw through the plan and determined to defeat it. He executed a rapid movement towards the Upper Danube valley and joined Prince Eugene near Ulm. Together they advanced to attack the enemy, and at Blenheim, a little village on the left bank of the Danube, a crushing defeat was inflicted upon the French and Bavarians. France never recovered the blow during the war. The whole electorate of Bavaria fell into the hands of the Allies. The empire was saved. *Battle of Blenheim, Aug. 13, 1704.*

In 1705 the chief interest of the fighting lies in Spain. The Earl of Peterborough captured and held Barcelona, and the entire district of Catalonia declared for Charles. Meanwhile in 1704 the English fleet, which had already seized a great squadron of Spanish treasure-ships in Vigo Bay, took Gibraltar, under the leadership of Sir John Rooke and Sir Cloudesley Shovel. *Campaigns in Spain.*

In 1706 the Allies triumphed on all three theatres of war. Marlborough broke into the French lines and crushed their armies a second time at Ramillies (May 23), securing the Netherlands, and occupying Brussels, Antwerp, Ghent, and Bruges. The French still held the barrier fortresses, chief of which were Mons, Tournai, and Lille; but they were obliged to keep to their own frontier instead of menacing that of Holland. In the same year Eugene succeeded in winning a victory at Turin, and thus prevented a diversion in favour of Louis in North Italy. The Empire, Holland, and Italy *A year of success.*

were now safe. It remained to see if the allies could seat their candidate in Spain. Here, too, there was success in that year. Barcelona was retained; Madrid was entered; yet the obstinate hostility of the Castilians was destined before long to render the position of the Allies in Spain quite untenable. Portugal was on their side, having been secured by the Methuen Treaty (1703), by which England consented to receive Portuguese wines at a less duty than French ones. This, though a useful alliance, had its disadvantage, in that Englishmen took to drinking port instead of claret. But, in spite of the gain of Portugal on one side of Spain and of Catalonia on the other, there still remained the all-important central provinces, whose animosity to the Allies and their candidate, Charles, could not be overcome. In 1707 the Duke of Berwick beat the Allies in the battle of Almanza, and confined them strictly to the small district round Barcelona, which had been true to them all along. There was little hope of a final triumph in Spain.

But Marlborough's career of victory went on unchecked. Baffled in their attack on Italy and on Austria, the French in 1708 made a vigorous effort to recover their hold on the Netherlands. But Eugene joined Marlborough, and a third signal victory was placed to the credit of the Allies at Oudenarde (July 11, 1708). The capture of Lille, the leading frontier fortress of France, soon followed.

Meanwhile in Scotland the oft-raised question of a Union with England had been settled at last. All through the century since James I.'s useless attempt the question had lain open. There were two great difficulties. The Scots absolutely refused all along to have anything to do with an Episcopal Church. The wretched failure of the Stewarts to force this upon them had been recognized by William as definite and never to be renewed. The separation of the two countries in church matters had been made absolute. Clearly, then, any political union must be one of state and not of church. Here the difficulty lay in matters commercial. English and Scottish merchants were

The Union with Scotland, 1707.

not on good terms. The Scots had to suffer the burden of the navigation laws as fully as if they had been Dutchmen. A parliamentary union might also be resisted by patriotic Scots, who liked to think of days when a handful of their race had beaten back the Plantagenet attack. But here there would not be much trouble. If religion were divided and commerce shared, the Union was likely to be easily accomplished. Under the rule of Cromwell Scotland had been united to England, and then all commercial restrictions had been removed. This free exchange ceased when, at the Restoration, the Scots Parliament regained its independence. They had, therefore, now to choose between independence and free trade. A scheme proposed by one Paterson, in the reign of William III., by which Scots were to secure a foremost place in the commercial world by colonizing the isthmus of Darien and making it a depôt for trade of east and west, had failed miserably. The Spaniards, whose rights they invaded, and the climate, which they thought much better than it proved to be, combined to kill off the colonists. This, together with the jealousy shown towards the enterprise in England, was enough to make a wider breach more probable than a closer union between the two nations.

But the Scots took advantage of the coming succession problem to make Englishmen think less of Scottish commercial rivalry and more of Scottish political union. Their parliament in Edinburgh declared in 1703 that, though they would have as sovereign after Queen Anne a descendant of the Electress Sophia, yet their nominee should not be the same as England's unless their religion and trade were secured. This "Act of Security" was indeed a skilful trick to bring the English to terms. Commissioners were named to discuss a union of the two realms, as soon as the northern kingdom threatened to sever the union of the two crowns, which had been a fact since 1603. The terms finally adopted were those we have suggested. Their religion was secured, their commerce made free:

The Act of Security.

their legal system remained to bear witness, if necessary, to their ancient independence: Scottish members, to the number of 45, were to sit in the House of Commons, while 16 peers were to be elected by the whole body of nobles to represent them in the House of Lords. Thus ended one of the greatest difficulties of the seventeenth century. We have seen how it baffled the wit of James I., brought Charles and Laud to war, and their system to overthrow. It had given occasion for the display of the cynical indifference of Charles II., and the bigoted brutality of his brother. Now prosperity and peace were to reward the Scots for a century of bloodshed and persecution.

Taking advantage of some considerable discontent when the independence of the kingdom was lost, the French and the Pretender tried in 1708 to create a diversion, by a Jacobite rising in Scotland. But the Pretender was delayed by the measles, and the French fleet was dispersed by the vigorous measures of Admiral Byng. Far from being recalled to defend England Marlborough was winning his fourth wonderful victory in September, 1709, by crushing Marshal Villars at Malplaquet. Mons fell, and the power of France was broken.

Malplaquet.

But this series of victories was over. In the second period of the reign the government was to be defeated at home though victorious abroad. For some time the Tory party, though weak, had been working to recover influence. They were led by Robert Harley, an ambitious and unscrupulous statesman, who, with Henry St. John, better known afterwards as Lord Bolingbroke, represented a Tory opposition to Marlborough and the war. The national feeling was now too important to be neglected, and every shift in it was eagerly watched by the Tories. They were not slow to note that the war, in spite of all its brilliant moments, was steadily waning in popularity; the taxation necessary to support it was heavy, and it was loudly asserted that Marlborough and the Whigs continued the war because it

A Tory reaction.

kept them in power. There were some grounds for such an assertion. More than once Louis had proposed to negotiate for a peace. He had even offered to give up assisting his grandson in Spain, to give the Dutch a number of barrier fortresses, and to banish the Pretender. But the Allies were not content: they insisted that the French king should help them to drive his grandson from Spain. They asked a half-conquered foe to join the Allies who had beaten him. This was too much; and France was stirred to enthusiasm by the imposition of terms which amounted to a national insult. This failure to make peace when it was offered on fair conditions exasperated many and caused a Tory reaction.

But another event in 1609 had even more effect. A high-church clergyman, named Dr. Sacheverell, attacked the Whigs and Dissenters from the pulpit, and went the length of publishing his sermons. *Dr. Sacheverell.* He spoke of the perils of the faithful among "false brethren", and described these latter in terms so clear that no one could mistake them. The government actually impeached this preacher, which was very foolish, for it gave him popularity among a far larger number of people than those who read the sermons in question. The man who had attacked and been attacked by the unpopular Whig government became a hero among Tories and churchmen, and the Tories gained from the enthusiasm which Sacheverell roused against the Whigs.

Meanwhile Harley was securing an ally at court whose services were more important still. Mrs. Masham, his cousin, was quietly gaining an influence over the mind of Anne which was soon to supplant *Mrs. Masham.* that of the duchess. The queen was tired of this tyrannous woman, and welcomed the more gentle sway of the new favourite.

Thus, with a Tory influence supreme at court and a Tory enthusiasm spreading in the street, the crisis of the war in 1710, when Louis' pro- *Fall of the war ministry, 1710.* posals were again refused at Gertruydenberg, led to a clean sweep of the Whig ministry. The queen had already refused to appoint Marlborough captain-general for life. The Tories came into power, and in the following year the great duke and his wife were dismissed from their offices. No pains were spared by the Tories to secure this triumph. They accused Marlborough of peculation under circumstances which do them little credit. They also secured the services of pamphleteers, foremost among whom was Dean Swift, the greatest prose writer of the age. In the *Conduct of the Allies* he attacked the war policy, and endeavoured to undermine the support which the Whigs possessed in the commercial interests of the nation: England, he urged, was getting terribly into debt in order to preserve Dutch towns, whose citizens would repay her by underselling English merchants. We were fighting for our rivals, not for ourselves. Our interest in the war was slight, yet we had become a chivalrous power willing to fight other people's battles all over Europe. Language like this had a great effect.

The Tory ministry marked its accession to power by an attack upon the Dissenters. They passed the famous bill against Occasional Conformity. It forbade men to receive the Sacrament, merely to qualify for office, and then go back to their Dissenting meeting-houses. The Tories hoped thus to exclude the Dissenting element from the town corporations, and through them from Parliament.

But the greatest achievement of the new ministers was the ending of the war by the Peace of Utrecht. They **Treaty of Utrecht, 1713.** had come to power as a peace ministry, protesting against the war and the war-makers. They now put an end to the struggle. The claimant for whom the Allies were fighting, the Archduke Charles, had become emperor about the time of the accession of the Tories to office. Their task was therefore easy. It was absurd to suppose that Spain was to be wrested from Louis and handed to the Emperor. Charles had been chosen as king when it was improbable that he would ever become emperor. It therefore remained to find another candidate and begin the war afresh, or to make peace. To leave Philip V. on the throne of Spain was certainly to give up an essential point. But as there was no one else, and as the Spaniards were not likely to accept any one else, it was a not altogether bad solution.

Louis therefore had the satisfaction of securing Spain for his grandson, and added a solemn engagement that the crowns of France and Spain should never be united, for the benefit of anyone who might still believe in solemn engagements. He acknowledged the Hanoverian succession, banished the Pretender, and restored to the Dutch their barrier fortresses. English merchants obtained some limited trading rights in the Spanish Indies. Finally, while England kept Gibraltar and Minorca, her colonial gains in the eighteenth century were foreshadowed by the acquisition of Newfoundland and other portions of French North America. The Netherlands and the Italian provinces of Milan, Sardinia, and Naples went to the emperor, the Duke of Savoy obtained Sicily, while Louis retained Strasbourg.

Thus, by 1713, the European question was settled and the triumph of party government had begun in England. It is noticeable that Tory peers were created specially to make a majority in the House of Lords in order to prevent opposition to the Peace.

In the third period of the reign the Succession question loomed large. Anne was in bad health. The Electress Sophia was over 80 years of age, and thus there was a near prospect of two rapid changes in the occupancy of the throne, if the latter should outlive the queen. *Danger to the Protestant succession.* Fortunately she died a few weeks earlier. Her son George, Elector of Hanover, was about fifty years of age and a good soldier, but beyond this little was known about him. The party spirit was so completely dominant in England that the Tory leaders may well have doubted whether such a king would be accepted by the nation. Harley, now Earl of Oxford, and his colleague Bolingbroke, are generally supposed to have intended to restore the Pretender, since they wrote letters to him. Perhaps they were only trimming, as better men had done before. But it seems that Bolingbroke at least had gone very far in the direction of conspiring for the restoration of James III. by force of arms. It is clear they had little to hope from the legal heir to the throne, who was sure to place power in the hands of the Whigs. Fortunately for England these two statesmen quarrelled just before Anne died. Oxford was dismissed. The question arose who should succeed him as Lord Treasurer. Some of the Whig lords promptly seized this opportunity of the Queen's illness, forced their way into the Privy Council, and secured the appointment of the Earl of Shrewsbury, a firm supporter of the Hanoverian succession. This decided the matter. Queen Anne died on August 1, 1714, and the Elector George Lewis was proclaimed King of Great Britain, France, and Ireland, Defender of the Faith.

The days of the Stewarts were over. Personal government by the monarch was now to become obsolete, under two foreign kings who knew nothing and cared nothing for English politics. For the first time in the history of the realm the sovereign was to become a secondary person in the governance of the land where he reigned but did not rule. His place was to be taken by the prime-minister, the chief of one of the party cabinets which were for the future to be the rule and not the exception. The next period of English history should be called the reign of Walpole, and not labelled with the comparatively insignificant names of the first two Georges. The ancient struggle between king and parliament had reached its end.

INDEX.

Abhorrers, the, 84.
Addresses, Vote of No, 57.
Adwalton Moor, battle of, 44.
Agitators, the, 56, 57, 60.
"Agreement of the People", 61.
Alford, battle of, 53.
Alliance, Triple, 76, 77.
Almanza, battle of, 122.
Alsace, coveted by Louis XIV., 75; occupied by him, 85.
America, Puritan colonists of, 74.
Anne, Queen, 82; excluded from the throne by Exclusion Bill, 84; reconciled to William III., 109; ruled by Countess of Marlborough, 109; accession of, 115, 120; character of, 116; dismisses the Churchills, 126; death, 127.
Argyle, Archibald Campbell, Marquis of, leader of Covenanters, 36, 58; executed, 76.
Argyle, Archibald, Earl of, son of above, rebels against James II., 90.
Arlington, Lord, member of the "Cabal", 76; concerned in Treaty of Dover, 77.
Arminianism, 23, and note.
Army, Standing, disliked, 76, 78, 80; disbandment of, demanded, 82; increased by James II., 91; established at Hounslow, 90.
Army, the New Model. See *Model*.
Array, Commissions of, issued by Charles I., 39.
Ashley, Anthony. See *Shaftesbury*.
Assembly, Glasgow, 29; Westminster, 48.
Assize, the Bloody, 91.
Association, the Eastern, 49.
Attainder, Bill of, against Strafford, 33.
Auldearn, battle of, 53.

Bacon, Sir Francis, 10; his theory of the judge's position, 12; disgrace of, 18.
Baillie, Robt., Scottish historian, 29, 50.
Bank of England founded, 107.
Barebones' Parliament, 64.
Bate, Case of Impositions, 10, 13.
Bavaria, Joseph, prince of, allotted Spain by the partition treaty, 112; dies, 113.
Bavaria, Elector of, joins the French, 120; beaten at Blenheim, 121.

Baxter, Richard, Presbyterian divine, 94.
Benevolence, a form of taxation, 13, 22.
Berwick, Duke of, wins battle of Almanza, 122.
Berwick, Pacification of, 30.
Bills, the Four, 57.
Bishops ejected from House of Lords, 38; restored, 72; Petition of the Seven, 95; their trial, 95.
Blake, Admiral, 63.
Blenheim, battle of, 121.
Bohemia rebels, 16; elects Frederick of the Palatinate as king, 16.
Bolingbroke, Henry St. John, Viscount, leader of the Tories, 124; intrigues with the Pretender, 127.
Bothwell Brig, battle of, 83.
Boyne, battle of the, 103.
Bradock Down, battle of, 44.
Breda, Declaration of, 69; Peace of, 75.
Brentford, sack of, 43.
Bridgewater stormed, 53.
Bristol, secured by Waller, 45; surrendered, 45; besieged by Fairfax and stormed, 54.
Buckingham, George Villiers, Duke of, 14, 17; influence over Charles I., 18; visit to Spain, 18; attacked in Parliament, 22; assassinated, 23.
Buckingham, George, Duke of, son of above, member of the "Cabal", 76.
Burgundy, County of, secured by Louis XIV., 75, 77, 81.
Byng, Admiral, disperses French fleet, 124.

Cabal, meaning of, 76, note; the administration of the, 76, 77; fall of, 78.
Cabinet, the, 6.
Cadiz, Expedition to, 22.
Cambridge, Vice-chancellor of, suspended by James II., 95.
Canons of 1604, 9.
Carr, Robert. See *Rochester* and *Somerset*.
Catesby the conspirator, 9.
Catharine of Braganza, wife of Charles II., 74.
Cavalier Parliament. See *Parliament*.
Cecil, Robert, Earl of Salisbury, minister of James I., 8; his policy and death, 11.
"Cessation", Irish, the, 48.

Chalgrove, battle of, 43.
Charles I., King of England, 4; proposed marriage with Spanish Princess, 13; visit of, to Spain, 18; accession of, 20; marriage, 20; character, 20; absolute rule of, 24; visits Scotland, 28; consents to Strafford's death, 33; visits Scotland, 34; reaction in favour of, 35; church policy, 36; his conservative attitude, 37, 38, 39; blunders in exciting suspicion, 38; his attempt on the Five members, 38; leaves London, 38; his military prospects, 41; failure of his cause, 52; his intrigues, 53; is pursued, 54; flies to Scottish camp, 54; seized by Cornet Joyce, 56; escapes to Isle of Wight, 57; trial and death of, 59.
Charles II., King of England: proclaimed in Edinburgh, 62; takes Covenant, 62; defeated at Worcester and escapes to France, 62; expelled from France, 66; issues Declaration of Breda, 69; restoration of, 69; character of, 70; his relations with Louis XIV., 71; his religious changes, 72; marriage, 73; his quarrel with Holland, 74; makes the secret Treaty of Dover, 77; issues Declaration of Indulgence, 77; opposition of Parliament to, 78, 80; applies to Louis XIV. for money, 81; defends his brother's succession, 82, 83, 85; secures a strong party, 85, 86; death, 87.
Charles II., King of Spain, designs of Louis XIV. on his kingdom, 75; dies, 112.
Charles, Archduke of Austria, candidate for the Spanish throne, 112; becomes Emperor, 126.
Cheriton, battle of, 49.
Chester, surrender of, 54.
Christ Church, Oxford, parliament in, 85; Roman Catholic appointed as Dean of, 95.
Churchill, John. See *Marlborough*.
Clarendon, Edward Hyde, Earl of, leader of church party in Long Parliament, 35; minister of Charles II. 73; fall of his administration, 76; impeached and banished, 76.
Clarendon, second Earl of, son of above, Lord-lieutenant of Ireland: dismissed by James II., 93.
Claverhouse, James Graham of, Viscount Dundee, heads Jacobite rising in Scotland, killed at Killiecrankie, 104.
Clifford, Sir Thomas, member of "Cabal", 76, 77.
Code, the "Clarendon", 73, 93.
Coke, Chief Justice, quarrel of, with James I., 10, 12, 13.

Colchester, Royalist rising at, 58.
Commission, Court of High, 26; abolished 34; revived, 92.
Commonwealth, the, 60.
Comprehension, meaning of, 72.
Compton, bishop of London: opposed to James II., 91, 92; suspended, 93; invites William to England, 96.
Conference, Hampton Court, 9, 26.
Conference, Savoy, 73.
Contract, the Great, 10.
Conventicle Act, the, 75.
Convention, the, of 1660, 69; character of its work, 71, 72; dissolution of, 72.
Convention of 1688, 97, 98, 102.
Corporation Act, 73.
Council, Privy, Temple's scheme for organizing, 82, 83.
Council of State during the Commonwealth, 61, 63.
Covenant, the Scottish, 29; the Solemn League and Covenant, 48.
Covenanters, persecution of, 76; defeat of, 83; proclaim William and Mary, 104.
Cromwell, Oliver, character of, 44; policy for organizing the Army, 46, 48; his raid round Oxford, 52; his campaign in the West, 54; attempts to come to terms with Charles, 56, 57; unpopular, 57; his part in Second Civil war, 58; his aims, 60; his campaign in Ireland, 61; in Scotland, 61; dissolves the "Rump", 63; becomes Protector, 64; opposed in Parliament, 65; his foreign policy, 66; refuses the title of king, 66; dies, 67.
Cromwell, Richard, son of above, becomes Protector, 67; his character and abdication, 67.
Culpeper, Sir John, 35, 48

Danby, Sir Thomas Osborne, Earl of, minister of Charles II., 79, 81; impeached, 81, 82; minister of William III., 103; his fall, 108.
Darien Scheme, the, 123.
Declaration of Indulgence. See *Indulgence*.
Devonshire, Earl of, opposes James II., 91, 96.
Digby, Sir Everard, conspirator, 9.
Digby, John, Earl of Bristol, ambassador in Spain under James I., 13, 18.
Dispensing Power, 74, note; use of, 89, 92; recognized by law, 92; James's abuse of, 92.
Dissenter, Letter to a, 94, note.
Dissenters, persecution of, 73; James II. and the, 93, 94.
Divine right, 4, 10, 70, 84, 87, 88.
Dover, Secret Treaty of, 77.

INDEX.

Drogheda, massacre at, 61.
Dunbar, battle of, 62.
Dundee. See *Claverhouse*.
Dunkirk, taken for England, 66; Sold to France, 74, 76.
Dutch, England's rivalry with, 14, 74; Cromwell's war with, 62, 64; designs of Louis XIV. against, 75, 76, 77; Charles II.'s wars with, 74, 75, 76, 77; peace with, 79.

Edgehill, battle of, 42.
Edinburgh, riot in, 28.
Eliot, Sir John, leads opposition in Parliament, 22; imprisonment and death of, 24.
Elizabeth, Queen, her church policy, 3.
Elizabeth, daughter of James I., her marriage, 11.
England, New, 26, 74.
Episcopacy, attacked in Long Parliament, 35.
✓ Eugene of Savoy, leader of Austrian army, 119; wins battle of Cremona, 121; joins Marlborough before Blenheim, 121; wins battle at Turin, 121; joins Marlborough before battle of Oudenarde, 122.
Exclusion Bill, 83, 84, 85.

Fairfax, Thomas, Lord, 44, 50; commands the New Model army, 51; campaigns of, 53, 54; marches on London, 56; his work in Second Civil war, 58.
Falkland, Lord, death of, 46.
Fawkes, Guy, 9.
Felton assassinates Buckingham, 23.
Ferdinand II., Emperor, 16.
Fire of London, 75.
Five Mile Act, 75.
Fleetwood demands independence of the army, 67.
Floyd, cruel punishment of, 17.
France, Buckingham allied with, 19; war with, 22; peace with, 24; alliance of Cromwell with, 66.
Frederick, Elector Palatine, marries daughter of James II., 11; elected King of Bohemia, 16; character of, 16.

✓ Gainsborough, battle of, 44.
George of Denmark, husband of Queen Anne, 116.
George, Elector of Hanover, becomes King of England, 127.
Gibraltar taken by the English, 121.
Glasgow, Assembly at, 29.
Glencoe, massacre of, 104.
Gloucester, siege of, 45, 46.
Godolphin, minister of William III., 103; of Anne, 120.
Gondomar, Spanish ambassador, 12, 16.

Goring, Lord, surrenders Portsmouth, 42; misconduct of, 53.
Graces, the, 25.
Grenville, Sir Bevil, 44.
Gustavus Adolphus, King of Sweden, 25.

Habeas Corpus Act, 83.
Hales, Sir Edward, case of, dispensing power, 92.
Halifax, George Savile, Lord, opposes Exclusion Bill, 83, 84; dismissed by James I., 91; his writings, 94, 95.
Hamilton, Marquis of, 36; leads Scots in Second Civil war, 58; executed, 62.
Hampden, John, resists Ship-money, 27; impeached, 38; killed, 43.
Harley, Robert, Earl of Oxford, leader of the Tories, 124; intrigues with the Pretender, 127.
Haslerigg, one of the Five members, 38.
Heidelberg, fall of, 17.
Henrietta Maria married to Charles I., 20; lands in England with money, 43
Henry IV. of France, death of, 11.
Henry, Prince of Wales, death of, 12.
Hereford surprised by Waller, 45; relief of, 54.
Hertford, Marquis of, 42, 44.
Hogue, La, battle of, 106.
Holles, one of the Five members, 38.
Hopton, Sir Ralph, victories of, 42-46; defeat of, 49, 54.
Hull, Charles refused admission to, 39.
Hyde, Anne, wife of James II., 82.
Hyde, Edward. See *Clarendon*.
Hyde, Lawrence, son of above. See *Rochester*.

Impositions, question of, 10, 13.
Incident, the, 36.
Indemnity, Bill of, 72, 102, 103.
Independents, 48; contrasted with Presbyterians, 52; success of, 52, 54; extreme party of, 64.
Indulgence, Declaration of, 1672, 77; withdrawn, 78.
Indulgence, Declaration of, 1687, 93; compared with that of 1672, 94; ordered to be read in church, 95.
Instrument of Government, the, 64.
Ireland, difficulties under James I., 11; Chichester's government of, 11; Strafford's government of, 25; rebellion of 1641, 36, 61; rising against the Commonwealth, 61; Jacobite rebellion in, 103.
Ireton, Henry, 61.

Jacobites, their intrigues against William III., 101; rising in Ireland, 103; in Scotland, 104; assassination plot against William III., 109.

Jamaica, capture of, 66.
James I., 4; character, 7; his problem, 7; his first parliament, 8, 10; religious policy, 9; quarrels with parliament, 8, 10, 17; quarrels with Coke, 10; foreign policy, 11, 12, 16, 19; his Spanish leanings, 14, 15, 17; death of, 19.
James II., scheme to exclude him from the throne, 82, 83, 84; his Roman Catholicism, 82, 89; marries Anne Hyde, 82; marries Mary of Modena, 82; his accession, 87; character and aims, 88, 89; his breach of Test Act, 91; opposition to him, 91; his measures to secure power, 92, 93; his attack on the universities, 95; birth of his son, 95; his escape, 97; his court at St. Germains, 101; heads rising in Ireland, 103; defeated and returns to France, 103; death, 114.
James, son of James II. See *Pretender*.
Jeffreys, Chief Justice, his Bloody Assize, 90, 91.
Jesuits, their influence at court of James II., 91, 93.
Jews allowed to return to England, 65.
Joyce, Cornet, seizes Charles I., 56.
Judges appealed to by Stewarts, 10.

Killiecrankie, battle of, 104.
Kilsyth, battle of, 52.
Kirke, Colonel, his cruelty, 90.

Lambert, John, General, leader of the Army, 64; demands independence for it, 67; deprived of his commission, 68; tried for treason, 73.
Langport, battle of, 53.
Lansdown, battle of, 45.
Laud, William, Archbishop of Canterbury, 21-25; character of, 21; his Arminian tendencies, 23; provokes resistance, 26; impeached, 32; executed, 51.
Lauderdale, member of the "Cabal", 76; governing in Scotland, 76.
Leicester sacked, 52.
Leslie, Alexander, 29.
Leslie, David, 53; defeats Montrose, 54.
Levellers, the, 57, 61, 68.
Limerick, siege of, 103.
Lindsey, Earl of, slain at Edgehill, 43.
London, petitions against Episcopacy, 35; anxious for peace, 45; fire of, 75; stronghold of the Whigs, 86; charter of, confiscated, 86; riots in, 93.
Londonderry, siege of, 103.
Lords, House of, abolished during Commonwealth, 61; restored at Restoration, 72; rejects Exclusion Bill, 85.
Lostwithiel, surrender of Essex at, 49.

Louis XIII., 20; secures English help against Huguenots, 22.
Louis XIV., his relations with Charles II., 71, 74; his European schemes, 75; war against England, 75; claims Spanish Netherlands, 76; Triple Alliance against, 76, 77; makes Treaty of Dover, 77; English opposed to, 78, 79; bribes English members of parliament, 80; his policy in England, 84, 85; paramount in Europe, 88; helps James II., 90; rescinds Edict of Nantes, 92; fails to prevent the invasion of William III., 96; receives James II., 101; his war with William III., 106; aids the Jacobites, 109; acknowledges William III. by Treaty of Ryswick, 110; his partition treaties, 112, 113; recognizes the Pretender as king of England, 115; war of Spanish Succession, 119-126; makes Treaty of Utrecht, 126.
Lunsford, Colonel, 37.

Magdalen College, Oxford, attacked by James II., 95.
Maidstone, Royalist rising at, 58.
Malplaquet, battle of, 124.
Manchester, Lord, 46, 50, 51.
Manifesto, the Army, 56.
Mansfield, Count, 17; his expedition, 19.
Maria, Infanta of Spain, proposed marriage of Charles I. to, 13.
Marlborough, John Churchill, Duke of, his intrigues with James II., 106; commands army in the Netherlands, 119, 120; wins battle of Blenheim, 121; of Ramillies, 121; of Oudenarde, 122; of Malplaquet, 124; dismissed from office, 126.
Marlborough, Sarah, Duchess of, her ascendancy over Queen Anne, 109, 120; dismissed, 126.
Marston Moor, battle of, 50.
Mary, Queen of Scots, 7.
Mary, daughter of Charles I., 74.
Mary, daughter of James II., married to William III., 80; excluded from throne by Exclusion Bill, 84; declared Queen by the Tories, 97; death, 108.
Mary of Modena, 82.
Masham, Mrs., her influence over Queen Anne, 125.
Matthias, Emperor, 15.
Maurice, Prince, 46, 48.
Mayflower, voyage of the, 26.
Methuen Treaty, the, 122.
Militia, the question of the control of, 37; demanded by parliament, 38; ordinance for regulating, 38, 39; declared to be in royal power, 72.
Millenary Petition, 9, 26.
Model, the New, 51; success of, 53;

INDEX.   133

becomes a political power, 56, 57, 58; remonstrance of, 59; quarrels with parliament, 63, 67, 68; disbanded, 72.
Monk, George, restores Charles II., 68.
Monmouth, James, Duke of, proposed as successor to Charles II., 83, 85; banished, 87; rebels against James II., 90; executed, 90.
Monopolies, 17, 28.
Montrose, Marquis of, opposes Argyle, 36; fights for Charles I., 50, 52, 53; defeated, 54; executed, 62.
Mutiny Act, the, 113.

Namur, capture of by the French, 107; retaken by William III., 109.
Nantes, Edict of, revoked, 92.
Naseby, battle of, 53.
Navigation Act, 62.
Netherlands, 11; Dutch, their truce with Spain, 11; Spanish, coveted by Louis XIV., 75, 76.
Newark, 44, 54.
Newburn, battle of, 31.
Newbury, first battle of, 46; second battle of, 51.
Newcastle, Scots retire to, 54; proposition of, 55.
Newcastle, Marquis of, 43; victories of, 44; danger of, 49; defeat of, 50.
Newmarket, 56.
Newport, Treaty of, 58.
Nimwegen, Peace of, 81.
Non-jurors, the, 102.

Oates, Titus, his perjuries, 81.
Occasional Conformity, bill against, 126.
Orange, William, Prince of, father of William III., 74.
Orange, William, Prince of. See *William III.*
Ordinance, militia, 38, 39; self-denying, 51.
Ormond, Duke of, 61.
Osborne, Sir Thomas. See *Danby.*
Oudenarde, battle of, 122.
Overbury, Sir Thomas, murdered, 14.
Oxford, head-quarters of Charles I., 43; treaty of, 45; surrender of, 54; parliament held at, 85.

Palatinate, loss of, 17.
Parliament, power of, in Tudor times, 6; quarrels with James I., 8, 10; intolerance of, 9.
— the Addled, 13; the Short, 30; the Mongrel, 48; Barebones', 64.
— the Long, meets, 32; work of, 34; disunion in, 35, 36; Puritan tendency of, 35; becomes revolutionary, 36; demands militia, 38; quarrels with Army, 56; claims sole legislative power, 59; dissolves itself, 69.

Parliament under Cromwell, packed, 66; refuses to accept a written constitution, 67.
— the "Cavalier", 71; its work, 72; persecutes Dissenters, 73; opposes Charles II., 77, 78; unpopularity of, 79, 81; dissolution of, 81.
— under James II., 90.
Parties, origin of English political, 84.
Partition Treaties, the, 112, 113.
Penal Laws, origin of, 8; question of, 14, 18, 19, 77, 89, 94.
Penn, William, 94.
Penruddock, rebellion of, 65.
Pensionary, Grand, 74.
Perpetuation Bill, 63.
Perth, Assembly at, 15; Five Articles of, 15, 29.
Petition and Advice, the, 66.
Petition of the Seven Bishops, 95.
"Petitioners", the, 84.
Petre, Father, 91.
Philip III. of Spain, 11, 13.
Philip IV. of Spain, 66.
Philip of Anjou, King of Spain, 113.
Philiphaugh, battle of, 54.
Pilgrim Fathers, the, 26, 74.
Plague, the Great, 75.
Plot, Gunpowder, 9; Popish, 81; Rye House, 86.
Portsmouth, 38; surrendered, 42.
Powick Bridge, battle of, 42.
Prague, battle of, 16.
Presbyterians, 7; organization of, 29; have majority in Parliament, 55; offer terms to Charles at Newport, 58; expelled from Parliament by Pride, 59; opposed to Cromwell, 66; restored to Parliament by Monk, 68; persecution of, 73, 89.
Preston, battle of, 58.
Pretender, the, son of James II., 95, 96; acknowledged King of England by Louis XIV., 115.
Pride, Colonel, purges Parliament, 59.
Propositions, the Ten, 34; the Nineteen, 39; of Newcastle, 55.
Protector, Cromwell becomes, 64.
Prynne, Puritan writer, 27, 32.
Purge, Pride's, 59.
Puritans, 2; origin of, 3; persecution of, 3; spirit of, 5; political importance of, 5, 40; demands of, 9, 23; division among, 48, 52.
Pym, John, 24, 30, 34, 37, 38, 48.
Pyrenees, Treaty of, 75.

Raleigh, Sir Walter, 2, 14.
Ramillies, battle of, 121.
Rebellion, the Great, results of, 70.
Recusancy, 8.
Reform of Constituencies during Commonwealth, 65.

Reformation, the, effect of, in England, 2, 3.
Regicides, punishment of, 72.
Remonstrance, the Grand, 37.
— of the Army, 59.
Republican party, 64, 66, 67.
Restoration, causes of the, 69, 70.
Revolution of 1688, 90, 98.
Rhé, Expedition to, 22.
Right, Declaration of, 98.
— Petition of, 23, 27.
Rights, Bill of, 98.
Ripon, Treaty of, 31.
Rochelle, 22.
Rochester, Lawrence Hyde, Earl of, 86, 91; dismissed, 93.
Roman Catholics, 2; persecuted, 3, 8, 9, 81, 89; Charles II. leans towards, 77, 80; James II. assists, 89, 94.
Root and Branch party, 35.
Rowton Heath, battle of, 54.
Rump, the, Parliament restored, 68; expelled, 68.
Russell, Admiral, wins battle of La Hogue, 106; his intrigues with James II., 106.
Russell, Lord William, leads Exclusion party, 82; executed, 87.
Russell, Edward, 96.
Rye House Plot, 86.
Ryswick, Treaty of, 110.

Sacheverell, his sermons against the Whigs, 125.
St. John, Henry. See *Bolingbroke*.
St. John, Oliver, prosecution of, 13.
St. Thomé burned by Raleigh's expedition, 14.
Saints, the, 64; Cromwell relies on them, 64.
Sancroft, Archbishop, 95; forfeits the archbishopric as a non-juror, 102.
Sarmiento. See *Gondomar*.
Savoy, Duke of, persecutes Protestants, 66.
Savoy Palace, Conference at, 73.
Schomberg, Marshal, sent by William III. to subdue rebellion in Ireland, 103.
Scotland, Union with England proposed, 8; rebellion of, against Charles I., 28; fights for Parliament, 48; army of, presents propositions to Charles I., 55; makes engagement with Charles I., 57; invades England, 58; rises against the Commonwealth, 61; forces of, beaten at Dunbar, 62; and at Worcester, 62; Jacobite rising in, 104; union with England, 122.
Scots anxious to convert England, 48, 49; make terms with Charles, 54.
Security, Act of, 123.
Sedgmoor, battle of, 90.

Selden, John, 52.
Settlement, Act of, 114.
Shaftesbury, Anthony Ashley Cooper, Earl of, 76; member of "Cabal"; advises the Declaration of Indulgence, 77; made Chancellor, 77; dismissed, 78; joins opposition, 78, 82, 83; his exclusion scheme, 84; tried for treason, 86; flies to Holland and dies, 86.
Ship-money, 25, 27, 34.
Shrewsbury, minister of William III., 103; lord-treasurer in 1714, 128.
Somers, John, Lord, his defence of the seven bishops, 95.
Somerset, Robert Carr, Earl of, 12, 14.
Sophia, Electress of Hanover, heiress to the throne of England, 114; death of, 127.
Sovereign power, 4; question of, raised, 5, 59; true solution of, 6; real question in the Civil war, 40; unsolved, 69; parties divided as to, 84; solution reached in 1688, 98.
Spain, James I. makes peace with, 11; objects of, 12; war with, 21; peace with, 24; campaigns in, 121, 122.
Spanish Succession, Problem of, 110; war of, 119-126.
Spice Islands, the, 14, 73.
Stamford, Lord, Parliamentary general, 44, 45.
Star Chamber, 13, 26, 27; abolished, 34.
Steenkerke, battle of, 106.
Stewart house, genealogy of, 111.
Strafford, Thomas Wentworth, Earl of, joins Charles I., 21; his policy, 21; in Ireland, 25; his advice about the Scottish rebellion, 29; his speech in Privy Council, 30, 32; impeached, 32; condemned by attainder, 33; executed, 34.
Strasbourg seized by Louis XIV., 86.
Stratton, battle of, 45.
Strode, William, 38.
Sunderland, Earl of, adviser of Charles II., 86.
Sweden joins Triple Alliance, 76.
Swift, Dean, his Tory pamphlets, 126.
Sydney, Algernon, executed, 87.

Tadcaster, battle of, 44.
Taunton, relief of, 52; crowning of Monmouth at, 90.
Taxation, arbitrary, 10, 13, 21, 24, 27, 34, 65.
Temple, Sir William, 82.
Test Act, 78, 91, 92.
Tests, 89; suspended, 94.
Tippermuir, battle of, 50.
Toleration, 6, 70, 77, 78, 79, 80, 84, 89, 90, 93, 97.
Toleration Act, the, 102.
Torbay, landing of William III. at, 96.

INDEX.

Tories, origin of, 84; victory of in Charles II.'s time, 85, 86; their difficulties at the Revolution, 97; policy of, under William III., 100, 107; under Anne, 117.
Treason, law of, 33, 87.
Triennial Act of 1641, 80.
Triennial Bill of 1693 vetoed by William III., 107; passed, 108.
Triers, Board of, appointed by Cromwell, 65.
Tromp, Admiral Van, 63.
Tunnage and Poundage, 21, 24.
Turnham Green, Charles I. at, 43.
Tyrconnel, Earl of, adviser of James II., 91; rules in Ireland, 93.

Ulster, Colonization of, 11.
Uniformity, Act of, 73.
Union, the, of England and Scotland, 8, 122, 124.
Utrecht, Treaty of, 126.
Uxbridge, Treaty of, 52.

Vane, Sir Harry, 33; executed, 73.
Verney, Sir Edmund, death of, 42.
Villars, Marshal, defeated at Malplaquet, 124.
Villiers. See *Buckingham*.
Virginia, Colony of, 74.

Waller, Sir William, 45, 48, 49, 50.
Wallingford House party, 67.
War, The Bishops', 31.
— The Great Civil, cause of, 40; nature of, 41.
— The Second Civil, 57, 58.
— The Thirty Years', 15, 16, 17, 25.
Wentworth, Sir Thos. See *Strafford*.
Wexford, storm of, 61.
Whigs, origin of, 84, 85, 86; ruin of, by Shaftesbury, 86; restored by James II.'s conduct, 88; victory of, in 1689, 97; their policy under William III., 100, 102, 107; their successes, 108-110; their policy under Anne, 117.
William III. kept from his office in Holland, 74; restored to it, 80; marriage, 80; opposes Louis XIV., 88; invited to England, 96; his difficulties, 96; lands at Torbay, 96; is made king, 98; his policy, 99; subdues rebellion in Ireland, 103; war with France, 101, 106, 107, 109; makes Peace of Ryswick, 112; partition treaties, 112, 113; death, 115; triumph of his policy, 115.
Winceby, battle of, 47.
Witt, de, 74, 75; murdered, 80.

York, attack upon Newcastle at, 49.
York, James, Duke of. See *James II.*

"The volumes contain the ripe results of the studies of men who are authorities in their respective fields."—THE NATION.

EPOCHS OF HISTORY

EPOCHS OF ANCIENT HISTORY
Eleven volumes, 16mo, each $1.00.

EPOCHS OF MODERN HISTORY
Eighteen volumes, 16mo, each $1.00.

The Epoch volumes have most successfully borne the test of experience, and are universally acknowledged to be the best series of historical manuals in existence. They are admirably adapted in form and matter to the needs of colleges, schools, reading circles, and private classes. Attention is called to them as giving the utmost satisfaction as class hand-books.

NOAH PORTER, *President of Yale College.*

"The 'Epochs of History' have been prepared with knowledge and artistic skill to meet the wants of a large number of readers. To the young they furnish an outline or compendium. To those who are older they present a convenient sketch of the heads of the knowledge which they have already acquired. The outlines are by no means destitute of spirit, and may be used with great profit for family reading, and in select classes or reading clubs."

CHARLES KENDALL ADAMS, *President of Cornell University.*

"A series of concise and carefully prepared volumes on special eras of history. Each is also complete in itself, and has no especial connection with the other members of the series. The works are all written by authors selected by the editor on account of some especial qualifications for a portrayal of the period they respectively describe. The volumes form an excellent collection, especially adapted to the wants of a general reader."

The Publishers will supply these volumes to teachers at SPECIAL NET RATES, and would solicit correspondence concerning terms for examination and introduction copies.

CHARLES SCRIBNER'S SONS, Publishers
153-157 Fifth Avenue, New York.

THE GREAT SUCCESS OF THE SERIES

is the best proof of its general popularity, and the excellence of the various volumes is further attested by their having been adopted as text-books in many of our leading educational institutions. The publishers beg to call attention to the following list comprising some of the most prominent institutions using volumes of the series:

Smith College, Northampton, Mass.
Univ. of Vermont, Burlington, Vt.
Yale Univ., New Haven, Conn.
Harvard Univ., Cambridge, Mass.
Bellewood Sem., Anchorage, Ky.
Vanderbilt Univ., Nashville, Tenn.
State Univ., Minneapolis, Minn.
Christian Coll., Columbia, Mo.
Adelphi Acad., Brooklyn, N. Y.
Earlham Coll., Richmond, Ind.
Granger Place School, Canandaigua, N. Y.
Salt Lake Acad., Salt Lake City, Utah.
Beloit Col., Beloit, Wis.
Logan Female Coll., Russellville, Ky.
No. West Univ., Evanston, Ill.
State Normal School, Baltimore, Md.
Hamilton Coll., Clinton, N. Y.
Doane Coll., Crete, Neb.
Princeton College, Princeton, N. J.
Williams Coll., Williamstown, Mass.
Cornell Univ., Ithaca, N. Y.
Illinois Coll., Jacksonville, Ill.

Univ. of South, Sewaunee, Tenn.
Wesleyan Univ., Mt. Pleasant, Ia.
Univ. of Cal., Berkeley, Cal.
So. Car. Coll., Columbia, S. C.
Amsterdam Acad., Amsterdam, N. Y.
Carleton Coll., Northfield, Minn.
Wesleyan Univ., Middletown, Mass.
Albion Coll., Albion, Mich.
Dartmouth Coll., Hanover, N. H.
Wilmington Coll., Wilmington, O.
Madison Univ., Hamilton, N. Y.
Syracuse Univ., Syracuse, N. Y.
Univ. of Wis., Madison, Wis.
Union Coll., Schenectady, N. Y.
Norwich Free Acad., Norwich, Conn.
Greenwich Acad., Greenwich, Conn.
Univ. of Neb., Lincoln, Neb.
Kalamazoo Coll., Kalamazoo, Mich.
Olivet Coll., Olivet, Mich.
Amherst Coll., Amherst, Mass.
Ohio State Univ., Columbus, O.
Free Schools, Oswego, N. Y.

Bishop J. F. HURST, *ex-President of Drew Theol. Sem.*

"It appears to me that the idea of Morris in his Epochs is strictly in harmony with the philosophy of history—namely, that great movements should be treated not according to narrow geographical and national limits and distinction, but universally, according to their place in the general life of the world. The historical Maps and the copious Indices are welcome additions to the volumes."

EPOCHS OF MODERN HISTORY.

A SERIES OF BOOKS NARRATING THE HISTORY OF ENGLAND AND EUROPE AT SUCCESSIVE EPOCHS SUBSEQUENT TO THE CHRISTIAN ERA.

Edited by
EDWARD E. MORRIS.

Eighteen volumes, 16mo, with 74 Maps, Plans, and Tables. Sold separately. Price per vol., $1.00.
The Set, Roxburgh style, gilt top, in box, $18.00.

THE BEGINNING OF THE MIDDLE AGES—England and Europe in the Ninth Century.
By the Very Rev. R. W. CHURCH, M.A.

"A remarkably thoughtful and satisfactory discussion of the causes and results of the vast changes which came upon Europe during the period discussed. The book is adapted to be exceedingly serviceable."—*Chicago Standard.*

"At once readable and valuable. It is comprehensive and yet gives the details of a period most interesting to the student of history."—*Herald and Presbyter.*

"It is written with a clearness and vividness of statement which make it the pleasantest reading. It represents a great deal of patient research, and is careful and scholarly."—*Boston Journal.*

THE NORMANS IN EUROPE—The Feudal System and England under the Norman Kings. By Rev. A. H. JOHNSON, M.A.

"Its pictures of the Normans in their home, of the Scandinavian exodus, the conquest of England, and Norman administration, are full of vigor and cannot fail of holding the reader's attention."—*Episcopal Register.*

"The style of the author is vigorous and animated, and he has given a valuable sketch of the origin and progress of the great Northern movement that has shaped the history of modern Europe."—*Boston Transcript.*

EPOCHS OF MODERN HISTORY

THE CRUSADES. By Rev. G. W. Cox.

"To be warmly commended for important qualities. The author shows conscientious fidelity to the materials, and such skill in the use of them, that, as a result, the reader has before him a narrative related in a style that makes it truly fascinating."—*Congregationalist.*

"It is written in a pure and flowing style, and its arrangement and treatment of subject are exceptional."—*Christian Intelligencer.*

THE EARLY PLANTAGENETS—Their Relation to the History of Europe; The Foundation and Growth of Constitutional Government. By Rev. W. Stubbs, M.A.

"Nothing could be desired more clear, succinct, and well arranged. All parts of the book are well done. It may be pronounced the best existing brief history of the constitution for this, its most important period."—*The Nation.*

"Prof. Stubbs has presented leading events with such fairness and wisdom as are seldom found. He is remarkably clear and satisfactory."—*The Churchman.*

EDWARD III. By Rev. W. Warburton, M.A.

"The author has done his work well, and we commend it as containing in small space all essential matter."—*New York Independent.*

"Events and movements are admirably condensed by the author, and presented in such attractive form as to entertain as well as instruct."—*Chicago Interior.*

THE HOUSES OF LANCASTER AND YORK—The Conquest and Loss of France. By James Gairdner.

"Prepared in a most careful and thorough manner, and ought to be read by every student."—*New York Times.*

"It leaves nothing to be desired as regards compactness, accuracy, and excellence of literary execution."—*Boston Journal.*

THE ERA OF THE PROTESTANT REVO-
LUTION. By FREDERIC SEEBOHM. With Notes, on Books in English relating to the Reformation, by Prof. GEORGE P. FISHER, D.D.

"For an impartial record of the civil and ecclesiastical changes about four hundred years ago, we cannot commend a better manual."—*Sunday-School Times.*

"All that could be desired, as well in execution as in plan. The narrative is animated, and the selection and grouping of events skillful and effective."—*The Nation.*

THE EARLY TUDORS—Henry VII., Henry VIII. By Rev. C. E. MOBERLEY, M.A., late Master in Rugby School.

"Is concise, scholarly, and accurate. On the epoch of which it treats, we know of no work which equals it."—*N. Y. Observer.*

"A marvel of clear and succinct brevity and good historical judgment. There is hardly a better book of its kind to be named."—*New York Independent.*

THE AGE OF ELIZABETH. By Rev. M. CREIGHTON, M.A.

"Clear and compact in style; careful in their facts, and just in interpretation of them. It sheds much light on the progress of the Reformation and the origin of the Popish reaction during Queen Elizabeth's reign; also, the relation of Jesuitism to the latter."—*Presbyterian Review.*

"A clear, concise, and just story of an era crowded with events of interest and importance."—*New York World.*

THE THIRTY YEARS' WAR—1618-1648.
By SAMUEL RAWSON GARDINER.

"As a manual it will prove of the greatest practical value, while to the general reader it will afford a clear and interesting account of events. We know of no more spirited and attractive recital of the great era."—*Boston Saturday Evening Gazette.*

"The thrilling story of those times has never been told so vividly or succinctly as in this volume."—*Episcopal Register.*

THE PURITAN REVOLUTION; and the First Two Stuarts, 1603-1660. By SAMUEL RAWSON GARDINER.

"The narrative is condensed and brief, yet sufficiently comprehensive to give an adequate view of the events related." —*Chicago Standard.*

"Mr. Gardiner uses his researches in an admirably clear and fair way"—*Congregationalist.*

"The sketch is concise, but clear and perfectly intelligible." —*Hartford Courant.*

THE ENGLISH RESTORATION AND LOUIS XIV., from the Peace of Westphalia to the Peace of Nimwegen. By OSMUND AIRY, M.A.

"It is crisply and admirably written. An immense amount of information is conveyed and with great clearness, the arrangement of the subjects showing great skill and a thorough command of the complicated theme."—*Boston Saturday Evening Gazette.*

"The author writes with fairness and discrimination, and has given a clear and intelligible presentation of the time."—*New York Evangelist.*

THE FALL OF THE STUARTS; and Western Europe. By Rev. EDWARD HALE, M.A.

"A valuable compend to the general reader and scholar." —*Providence Journal.*

"It will be found of great value. It is a very graphic account of the history of Europe during the 17th century, and is admirably adapted for the use of students."—*Boston Saturday Evening Gazette.*

"An admirable handbook for the student."—*The Churchman.*

THE AGE OF ANNE. By EDWARD E. MORRIS, M.A.

"The author's arrangement of the material is remarkably clear, his selection and adjustment of the facts judicious, his historical judgment fair and candid, while the style wins by its simple elegance."—*Chicago Standard.*

"An excellent compendium of the history of an important period."—*The Watchman.*

THE EARLY HANOVERIANS—Europe from the Peace of Utrecht to the Peace of Aix-la-Chapelle. By EDWARD E. MORRIS, M.A.

"Masterly, condensed, and vigorous, this is one of the books which it is a delight to read at odd moments; which are broad and suggestive, and at the same time condensed in treatment."—*Christian Advocate.*

"A remarkably clear and readable summary of the salient points of interest. The maps and tables, no less than the author's style and treatment of the subject, entitle the volume to the highest claims of recognition."—*Boston Daily Advertiser.*

FREDERICK THE GREAT, AND THE SEVEN YEARS' WAR. By F. W. LONGMAN.

"The subject is most important, and the author has treated it in a way which is both scholarly and entertaining."—*The Churchman.*

"Admirably adapted to interest school boys, and older heads will find it pleasant reading."—*New York Tribune.*

THE FRENCH REVOLUTION, AND FIRST EMPIRE. By WILLIAM O'CONNOR MORRIS. With Appendix by ANDREW D. WHITE, LL.D., ex-President of Cornell University.

"We have long needed a simple compendium of this period, and we have here one which is brief enough to be easily run through with, and yet particular enough to make entertaining reading."—*New York Evening Post.*

"The author has well accomplished his difficult task of sketching in miniature the grand and crowded drama of the French Revolution and the Napoleonic Empire, showing himself to be no servile compiler, but capable of judicious and independent criticism."—*Springfield Republican.*

THE EPOCH OF REFORM—1830-1850. By JUSTIN MCCARTHY.

"Mr. McCarthy knows the period of which he writes thoroughly, and the result is a narrative that is at once entertaining and trustworthy."—*New York Examiner*

"The narrative is clear and comprehensive, and told with abundant knowledge and grasp of the subject."—*Boston Courier.*

IMPORTANT HISTORICAL WORKS.

CIVILIZATION DURING THE MIDDLE AGES. Especially in its Relation to Modern Civilization. By GEORGE B. ADAMS, Professor of History in Yale University. 8vo, $2.50.

Professor Adams has here supplied the need of a text-book for the study of Mediæval History in college classes at once thorough and yet capable of being handled in the time usually allowed to it. He has aimed to treat the subject in a manner which its place in the college curriculum demands, by presenting as clear a view as possible of the underlying and organic growth of our civilization, how its foundations were laid and its chief elements introduced.

Prof. KENDRIC C. BABCOCK, University of Minnesota:—"It is one of the best books of the kind which I have seen. We shall use it the coming term."

Prof. MARSHALL S. BROWN, Michigan University:—"I regard the work as a very valuable treatment of the great movements of history during the Middle Ages, and as one destined to be extremely helpful to young students."

BOSTON HERALD:—"Professor Adams admirably presents the leading features of a thousand years of social, political, and religious development in the history of the world. It is valuable from beginning to end."

HISTORY OF THE UNITED STATES. By E. BENJAMIN ANDREWS, D.D., LL.D., President of Brown University. With maps. Two vols., crown octavo, $4.00.

BOSTON ADVERTISER:—"We doubt if there has been so complete, graphic, and so thoroughly impartial a history of our country condensed into the same space. It must become a standard."

ADVANCE:—"One of the best popular, general histories of America, if not the best."

HERALD AND PRESBYTER:—"The very history that many people have been looking for. It does not consist simply of minute statements, but treats of causes and effects with philosophical grasp and thoughtfulness. It is the work of a scholar and thinker."

www.ingramcontent.com/pod-product-compliance
Lightning Source LLC
Chambersburg PA
CBHW030350170426
43202CB00010B/1318